BASERUNNING

Mike Roberts

with

Tim Bishop

Human Kinetics

Library of Congress Cataloging-in-Publication Data

Roberts, Mike, 1950-
  Baserunning / Mike Roberts, Tim Bishop.
    pages cm
1. Base running (Baseball) I. Title.
  GV868.R62 2013
  796.357'27--dc23

                                        2013031650

ISBN-10: 1-4504-3218-2 (print)
ISBN-13: 978-1-4504-3218-4 (print)

The web addresses cited in this text were current as of October 2013, unless otherwise noted.

Acquisitions Editor: Justin Klug; **Developmental Editor:** Cynthia McEntire; **Assistant Editor:** Elizabeth Evans; **Copyeditor:** Mark Bast; **Graphic Designer:** Fred Starbird; **Cover Designer:** Keith Blomberg; **Photograph (cover):** William Purnell/Icon SMI; **Photographs (interior):** © Human Kinetics; **Photo Asset Manager:** Laura Fitch; **Visual Production Assistant:** Joyce Brumfield; **Photo Production Manager:** Jason Allen; **Art Manager:** Kelly Hendren; **Associate Art Manager:** Alan L. Wilborn; **Illustrations:** © Human Kinetics; **Printer:** United Graphics

We thank the Cotuit Kettleers in Cotuit, Massachusetts, for assistance in providing the location for the photo shoot for this book.

Human Kinetics books are available at special discounts for bulk purchase. Special editions or book excerpts can also be created to specification. For details, contact the Special Sales Manager at Human Kinetics.

Printed in the United States of America   10 9 8 7 6 5 4 3 2 1

The paper in this book is certified under a sustainable forestry program.

Human Kinetics
Website: www.HumanKinetics.com

United States: Human Kinetics
P.O. Box 5076
Champaign, IL 61825-5076
800-747-4457
e-mail: humank@hkusa.com

Canada: Human Kinetics
475 Devonshire Road Unit 100
Windsor, ON N8Y 2L5
800-465-7301 (in Canada only)
e-mail: info@hkcanada.com

Europe: Human Kinetics
107 Bradford Road
Stanningley
Leeds LS28 6AT, United Kingdom
+44 (0) 113 255 5665
e-mail: hk@hkeurope.com

Australia: Human Kinetics
57A Price Avenue
Lower Mitcham, South Australia 5062
08 8372 0999
e-mail: info@hkaustralia.com

New Zealand: Human Kinetics
P.O. Box 80
Torrens Park, South Australia 5062
0800 222 062
e-mail: info@hknewzealand.com

E5783

BASERUNNING

Contents

Foreword

It might seem strange that I'm writing a foreword to a book on baserunning. After all, in my playing days, I wasn't known for my blazing speed or success for swiping a bag, although in 10 years, I racked up an impressive 12 stolen bases in 24 attempts. But whether it was my early days in Montreal watching the great Tim Raines, or as a coach in the minor and major leagues, I realized rather quickly the impact smart, aggressive baserunning has on a game, team, and season.

Successful baserunning requires more than speed. Though speed certainly helps, the fact is that the mental attitude and physical skills can be coached, developed, and perfected regardless of how fast a player may be. Take, for example, Dustin Pedroia, who I had the opportunity to coach while I was manager of the Boston Red Sox. If you look at his statistics, you might think he's just exceptionally fast, but that is simply not the case. Instead his incredible instincts and baserunning skills make him one of the biggest game changers in baseball. One coach who has demonstrated the ability to develop such players time and time again is Mike Roberts. When it comes to baserunning, he is the best in the game.

I first met Mike in 1976. I was playing high-school baseball at New Brighton High School, just outside Pittsburgh, Pennsylvania. During my high-school years, I was fortunate enough to be highly recruited by several college baseball programs. One of the first programs to recruit me was the University of North Carolina. Today the Tar Heels are well known for their on-field success every year, but back when I was recruited, they were in a rebuilding phase. The head coach tasked with bringing the program back to prominence was Mike Roberts.

I recall my official visit in the fall of 1976, my junior year of high school. The Roberts family opened their home to me and treated me as if I was part of the family. At that time, Mike's daughter Angie was only three years old, and I found myself sitting on the floor playing with her and thinking about how impressed I was that a coach of a big time university would actually go out of his way to make me feel so welcomed. As part of the recruiting process, I had the chance to see a North Carolina basketball game coached by the great Dean Smith. Between going to the game and spending time with Mike's family, I was so impressed through my visit that I signed a Conference Letter of Intent with UNC.

Unfortunately, at the beginning of my senior high-school season I suffered a knee injury that would keep me out for the remainder of the season. I remember talking to Mike on the phone from my hospital room, and he assured me that my scholarship status was in no way in jeopardy. As with any athlete coming out of high school, I was still being recruited by other schools. One of those schools recruiting me was the University of Arizona and coach Jerry Kindall. As I weighed my options, I realized that I was going to have to make one of the most difficult phone calls of my life—a call to Mike to inform him that I had decided that it was in my best interest to sign a National Letter of Intent with Arizona.

Although I never had the chance to play for Mike Roberts, he taught me many important lessons through my recruitment about respect and integrity. As my baseball career progressed, I learned many other baseball lessons by following his teams and, let me tell you, when it comes to running the bases, there isn't another coach out there with the same level of expertise! The work he puts in every day of every year working with players from the youth level to college and professional level is a true testament of his dedication to the sport and desire to affect the lives of those he works with. If you want to become a dynamic threat on the bases, you have come to the right place! This is not just another run-of-the-mill instructional resource. Rest assured that anything baseball-related that Mike Roberts attaches his name to is going to be the premier resource of its kind.

Now as manager of the Cleveland Indians, I still appreciate the opportunity to stay in touch with Mike. Even though I never played for UNC, Mike continues to be a valuable source of knowledge for me as well as for coaches around the country. I speak as a former recruit and player and now as a fellow coach, colleague, and friend when I say that whether you are playing in a community league or high school, college, or professional ranks, or if you happen to coach one of these teams, Mike Roberts' book is an absolute must-have! I have been fortunate throughout my career to be around some great baserunning coaches, and Mike is right at the top of that list. There's much more than just speed to running the bases, and *Baserunning* will give you everything you need to be a serious threat every time you reach base!

Terry Francona
Manager, Cleveland Indians

Acknowledgments

I would like to dedicate this book to three gentlemen—Edd Roberts, John Whited, and Jim Herbert—who were my role models and baseball coaches as I was growing up in Kingsport, Tennessee. They taught me to always hustle on the baseball field; practice, practice, and practice more the fundamentals correctly; cherish every day I had the opportunity to wear a baseball uniform; and make sure to represent myself in a first-class manner on and off the field.

Edd Roberts, my father, spent an incredible number of hours playing catch with me in the yard and teaching the baseball fundamentals that I still embrace today. He wanted all the local youngsters to have an opportunity to play baseball, enjoy decent fields to play on (that meant not too many rocks on dirt infields in the 1950s and '60s), and uniforms to wear each summer. To make this happen, Dad would go door to door to local businesses each year to raise money so we could have summer baseball teams. I will always be grateful to him for helping so many young players have a positive experience in baseball.

Coach John Whited, my coach at Dobyns-Bennett High School in Kingsport, Tennessee, taught me to play the game with such passion that anyone watching knew his players loved to play. They knew he loved to coach. That passion for the game is still in my soul today. Coach had such a positive influence on hundreds of baseball athletes at Dobyns-Bennett High School, at East Tennessee State University where he became an assistant coach, and at the University of Tennessee where he completed his career as an assistant coach and eventually head coach.

Jim Herbert was a pitcher at the University of Tennessee and an engineer at Tennessee Eastman Kodak in Kingsport. Mr. Herbert became a volunteer in the youth programs in town when he was in his early 20s and continued working with youth baseball players for 50-plus years. Even after athletes had graduated from high school and left the area to play in college, Coach would drive to many campuses to watch them play. When I was fortunate to coach teams that played in the NCAA Division I College World Series in Omaha, Nebraska, he traveled to support my team. I will always appreciate this incredible loyalty and dedication.

Key to Diagrams

P	Pitcher
C	Catcher
1B	First baseman
2B	Second baseman
3B	Third baseman
SS	Shortstop
B	Batter
R	Runner
X	Any player, if position isn't applicable

———————▶ Path of runner

- - - - ▶ Path of ball

················· Imaginary line for leads

Part One

Basepath Fundamentals

Excellent fundamentals on the basepaths make every base runner and base stealer look as comfortable as if he were enjoying a jog on the beach or dancing on a stage. The athlete looks faster, quicker, and lighter on his feet when returning to the base, turning to run, sliding, or just taking an ordinary lead.

Athletes should develop their own basepath philosophy, with help from coaches, after learning fundamental techniques and then gaining experience on the basepaths. Helping young baseball players develop a baserunning philosophy is something coaches should do but has often been omitted from coaching. The improved mind-set of an experienced base runner once he reaches base is so important and will lead to better results.

Players who enjoy practicing their running form seem to always improve running times, whether in a straight line or around the bases. This kind of practice is diligent work. All players will find they need to make big or subtle changes and will benefit from spending time looking at pictures and video in detail to find their flaws and then go back to work.

Overall, baseball players have lost their love of sliding and actually liking to get dirty. The game of baseball was built in the 1800s on dust bowl fields with rocks and undulations and tearing of pants or uniforms as players slid. In the early 1900s, Ty Cobb was a terror on the basepaths, sending dust flying after each slide. Players in today's game need to regain that aggressive mentality as they go into a base. Each slide described in part one should be practiced aggressively and to fundamental perfection. Players will hear safe calls on close plays more often as they learn the best way to touch the base with their foot or hand.

Leads should be practiced whenever an offensive player takes the field, whether in practice or on game day. Repetitions are a must for athletes to become comfortable with many styles and lengths of leads. As players practice their leads, fundamentals get better, size and variations of leads improve, possible pickoffs are not even a concern, and every athlete will improve his rhythm and grace.

More Than Speed

Successful baserunning is never just talent, never just speed. It requires a passion for running and stealing bases, dirtying the uniform, creating some chaos, playing the "game inside the game" full speed, and finding ways on the basepaths to help your team.

Several people, both lay coaches and full-time coaches, influenced the development of my coaching philosophy on baserunning and base stealing. These coaches gave me the foundation on which to build a complete coaching philosophy. That helped me develop the confidence to venture into one or two particular areas of the game that would become my passion and the core of my game philosophy.

COACHING PHILOSOPHY

Do coaches need a philosophy? Does it take a core philosophy and detailed understanding to have athletes buy in? If asked, can a coach describe his philosophy in an organized but detailed manner? If needed, can he actively teach and demonstrate parts or all of his philosophy? Does he have a mentor to help build or strengthen his philosophy?

When I was young, I learned the many aspects of the game of baseball from my father working with me in the backyard and as I tagged along to watch him coach his Little League team. Even though my dad never played organized baseball, he had an incredible feel for some areas of the game that many coaches ignored. One of those areas I embraced from him was his love of having fun when running the bases. My dad believed a uniform should look good and be fairly comfortable, but its true purpose was skin protection so a player could always slide or dive somewhere on the field. When the game was complete and the player started home, his uniform should be dirty or covered in grass stains.

Dad taught me to take advantage of any time I reached base. He encouraged me to do all I could to find a way to move myself into a better scoring position. I was taught to distract the pitcher and hope he made an errant pickoff attempt, attempt to steal a base to force the catcher into a wild throw, and make infielders pay attention to what I was doing to get them out of position. I wanted to move myself around the bases and try to score without the aid of a teammate's base hit.

He wanted young players to be aggressive in all areas of the game but especially when running the bases. Dad encouraged me to run the bases full speed, take an extra base whenever possible, and bring a cloud of dust when sliding into a base. There was no doubt that reading about the way Hall of Famer Ty Cobb ran the bases influenced my father.

Dad made practicing and playing baseball fun. It did not matter whether we were playing catch in the yard or watching him teach young players how to play the game all-out in an organized setting. I always looked forward to the next game of catch or opportunity to be at the field.

TEACHING DETAILED BASERUNNING AND BASE STEALING

When I was old enough to play on my father's Optimist Little League team, which allowed kids aged 9 to 12, I was the catcher many games but also did some pitching and on offense was the lead-off hitter. The team played in the town's recreational department league, which was very competitive in a small southern community. The town league played the complete adult version of the game of baseball, which meant we could steal bases at any age. There were no leagues in the area in which players had to keep one foot on the base until the ball was thrown by the pitcher. This helped players to embrace each aspect of the game and try to keep improving individually as the team worked to improve collectively.

Young pitchers were motivated to learn to hold runners on base. Catchers were challenged to throw quickly and accurately. Before I was 10 years old, I had to practice many hours with my catch and release to learn to throw out runners trying to steal. Infielders learned to focus on each pitch and communicate with their teammates so they would be prepared to cover a base, catch the ball, and make a tag while on the move. If teams in our league could not handle the running game, it became a track meet on the basepaths, and scores skyrocketed.

Each practice was important in helping players improve and teams become cohesive in their overall play. Young players were shown that practicing improves the offensive and defensive side of the running game. I learned that practice through repetition was the key to being able to execute and that athletes must practice often, certainly much more than they play.

My practice philosophy is built on repetition and exaggeration. Athletes must put more hours into practice than games. Coaches should schedule a minimum of twice as many practices as games played.

My father's philosophy was that a team should practice a minimum of two times before each game or double the number of hours it took to play a game. So if a team played 20 games in a season and the average game took 2 hours, for a total of about 40 hours of game time, then there should be at least 40 practices, totaling 80-plus hours of practice time. All athletes have a good chance of improving their game, regardless of athletic skills, with this amount of high-quality practice time.

The first practice after a game was primarily used for reviewing how the team played in the previous game. Dad would emphasize the areas of the game in which the team performed well but also work on areas in which some or all team members struggled with execution. The second practice ensured we were all working together with a positive approach as the team prepared for the next game. Our practices involved lots of fun, and we looked forward to each one.

Through my father's teaching, which came from his instincts and not playing experience, and then later from that of my high school coach John Whited, whose teaching gifts came from his instincts and a great deal of playing experience, I formed the basis of my teaching beliefs. I found joy in the daily teaching of baseball's fundamentals. However, my passion became base stealing and baserunning.

At the conclusion of each high school season during my playing days, Coach Whited would hang up the hat or pants or maybe the entire uniform of the grubbiest player from that year and leave it hanging in the locker room until the next season began. I was fortunate to have some of my gear hanging up for three consecutive years. Since I had average ability, I had to find a way to help my team each game, so I was always diving and sliding on both offense and defense.

Coach Whited was an outstanding practice and game coach. By the end of my high school career, mainly because I had enjoyed playing for Coach Whited so much, I decided I eventually wanted to coach full time after my playing days were completed. I developed this philosophical statement by the time I entered college: Practices are for coaches to teach and for players to learn. Games are for players to have fun and coaches to see if players can execute.

Coaches need to ask whether they are budgeting enough practice time to teach effectively. Are they teaching baserunning and base stealing at each base in detail? Are they teaching at a slow, rhythmic pace with every movement done precisely? Are they allowing enough repetitions so the player can make a smooth transition to the game?

In today's baseball world it is rare for amateur or professional teams to practice more than they play. A philosophy of good practice throughout the United States has deteriorated greatly. Youth teams (now known more as travel teams) like to play many more hours than they practice. Professional teams, except for spring training, never practice and rarely take infield before a game.

Primer for Teaching Baserunning and Base Stealing

- ◆ Make it a part of practice every day.
- ◆ Prepare fun drills at a different base each day.
- ◆ Make some drills competitive.
- ◆ Experiment.
- ◆ Teach by exaggeration.

PHILOSOPHY FOR COACHING A SUMMER BASEBALL TEAM

Summer is player separation time. It's time to find out who plays because he loves the game and who plays because others love to see him play the game. Which athletes will put in the practice repetition time, and which are just putting in time? It's time to teach how to get down and dirty on the basepaths and learn how to dominate a game!

My first venture into head coaching was after I retired from professional baseball and returned to graduate school at the University of North Carolina. I was given the opportunity at 24 years of age to be the head coach of the team the university placed in the North Carolina Collegiate Summer League. This allowed me to continue to develop my overall coaching philosophy.

When I began coaching summer baseball, I held two-a-day practices for several days before the season opened. This came from my playing high school football and going through two-a-day practices to learn how to block and tackle. We used this time to focus on fundamentals before we even thought about playing a game together as a team.

In the best-selling book *The Last Lecture* (2008, Hyperion), Dr. Randy Pausch talks about his Little League football practice experience with Coach Graham. The kids were scared at the first practice because he was old-school tough. Coach Graham asked, "How many men are on the football field at a time?" The players answered 11. Coach Graham then said, "That makes 22 on the field at any given time. And how many people are touching the football at any given time?" A player answered, "One of them." "Right!" the coach said. "So we're going to work on what those *other* 21 guys are doing." Dr. Pausch remembers Coach Graham's philosophy of fundamentals: "That was a great gift Coach Graham gave us."

In my initial season as head coach, I learned to use the afternoon before a game more wisely by setting up individual work with athletes in 90-minute practice sessions on fundamentals. This teaching occurred before the entire team met for loosening up and the normal pregame routine, and it enabled me to find out which summer players were playing to improve and which were just playing. I certainly hear more whining from a few players today than I did several years ago because of the amount of time this takes. Current players like to play more for the glory of one big play than cherish each play as the game progresses.

I enjoy the opportunity to work with athletes who embrace practicing as much as they like being seen in games. Potential team leaders like entering the field for practice, have a better understanding of the purpose of daily practice, and can see how practice through repetition helps their game. During practice, I search for these leaders who will motivate their teammates to stay more focused, communicate, and execute during games.

My work habits and teaching philosophy come from the mentors I had during my childhood in the 1950s and '60s, when coaches emphasized to players the need to show improvement and respectable execution in practice before they could possibly play in a game, much less execute in one. This is called skill development and polishing those skills.

I played for coaches who would hold an athlete out of a game if he was sloppy in practice and did not take practicing seriously. For coaches to develop more confidence in an athlete, they need to see a player trying to improve the small areas of the game in practice. The game is won or lost in the details!

I was influenced greatly by two college basketball coaches known for their detailed teaching of fundamentals, John Wooden at UCLA and Dean Smith at the University of North Carolina. These coaches silently helped me develop my teaching philosophy as I began my full-time coaching career. Dean Smith once said, "Play hard; play together; play smart! Focus on the effort and the end will take care of itself . . . create a system that demands effort, rewards it, and punishes its absence . . . execute properly; understand and consistently execute the fundamentals; drill the fundamentals!" John Wooden noted, "Be observing constantly; stay open minded; be eager to learn and improve; have knowledge of and the ability to properly and quickly execute the fundamentals; be prepared and cover every little detail."

Both Wooden and Smith began their collegiate coaching careers in the late 1950s and early 1960s. Coach Wooden and Coach Smith rarely allowed any athlete's talent to determine when he played, how much he played, and how he played the game. Each athlete in their programs, whether talented or just average, was required to learn the fundamentals in practice well before he played in games. This pushed each player to earn the opportunity to play alongside another no matter his talent level. These coaching legends' teaching philosophies were the main reason both were consistently successful at a Hall of Fame level.

Coach Smith had many great players who went on to play in the NBA, as did Coach Wooden. Michael Jordan was the greatest offensive player Coach Smith ever had on his roster. Obviously, we will never know if Michael could have been the greatest scorer in UNC basketball history because under Coach Smith the importance of one person scoring a lot of points was way down the list. Steve Previs, one of Coach Smith's former players, said, "It was all about *we*, not *me*. It was the thread that wove us together."

There was a saying during Michael's playing days at the University of North Carolina, 1982 to 1984, that criticized Coach Smith for his philosophy on only one player scoring: "The only person who can keep Michael Jordan from scoring is Coach Smith!" Coach Smith wanted Michael to be a complete player. Smith wanted Michael's defense at as high a level as his offensive skills. The reason behind this saying was Coach Smith's belief in the team game and working hard to be above average in every area of the game so that one person scoring a lot of points just wasn't necessary.

I watched Michael in practice several times work on his defense in great detail. Coach Smith teaching him the fundamentals in all areas helped Michael become an all-star on defense as well as offense. As stated earlier, fundamentals in all areas of an athlete's game should come first. Then eventually a more polished player can evolve.

One of my goals is to help create a complete player. A large piece of that creation is teaching every baseball player that he has the ability to be an outstanding base runner and can have excellent mental and physical talents for base stealing.

BASERUNNING AND BASE-STEALING PHILOSOPHY

Credit for igniting my passion for the game and helping mold my baserunning and base-stealing philosophy goes to the dedicated and experienced coaching staff at the Kansas City Baseball Academy in Sarasota, Florida. The academy was started in 1968 by Ewing Kauffman, former owner of the Kansas City Royals. I was fortunate to spend six weeks at this academy during the early summer of 1972.

The Kansas City Baseball Academy was the first boarding baseball academy developed in the United States. Its primary purpose was research and development with young players who had actually played little or no baseball up through their high school years. As I visited and then participated in the academy, I was involved in a lot of trial and error regarding running the bases and base stealing. This was a tremendous experience for a young man who thought he wanted to coach after his professional playing days.

The coaches at the academy had a passion for teaching fundamentals similar to the way my father, Coach Whited, Coach Smith, and Coach Wooden did. It felt like baseball heaven. As a catcher, I was practicing my throws to the bases each day, running the bases full speed as we experimented with how much to rely on coaches, and working on my base stealing in live situations with pitchers, catchers, and position players. During games at the academy, I saw up close how fundamentally sound baserunning and well-executed base stealing can positively affect almost every game played.

Steve Boros, one of the coaches at the KC Academy, said years after the academy closed while he was still coaching professionally, "A day does not go by where I don't use the things I learned at the academy. It's the foundation for the way I evaluate a player." After my KC Royals academy experience, I was hooked for life on teaching all aspects of baserunning. I remain passionate many years later in coaching any aspect of baserunning or base stealing.

With baserunning, I enjoy watching my players or their opponents running around the bases in a rhythmic sprint and instinctively making decisions with minimal help from coaches. With base stealing, I enjoy seeing baseball players as comfortable off the base as standing on it when taking and understanding how to vary leads. These players are polished enough in their base-stealing abilities to rotate the game in their direction.

PLAYER MIND-SET

Coaches must get athletes excited about learning to dominate the basepaths individually and as a team. To accomplish this, stress baserunning daily, instilling into players' minds that comfort off a base, comfort with body movement and technique, and instincts are just as important in maneuvering around the bases as speed.

Are coaches gaining the mind-set of their athletes? Are athletes gaining confidence as they learn details on the bases? Are you developing a team philosophy for baserunning and base stealing? Is every athlete, regardless of speed, learning ways to be effective on the bases? Are athletes learning how to work together if they are on the bases at the same time?

Coaches must gain the athlete's confidence and mind-set early on. They have to get players excited to run the bases and work on base stealing in practice. When players are excited and want to learn more, coaches should teach the smallest details of picking up advantages on the basepath. This improves the athlete's comfort and instincts and leads to quick improvement.

My son Brian loved to run and always wanted to start up a game of pickle in the yard, at the beach, or wherever he could find a ball and a couple of people to play with him. Syd Thrift, director of the KC Academy, always said, "The most effective instruction is repetitive." I believe the reason Brian became an exceptional base runner and base stealer was repetition.

In pickle, bases are placed approximately 20 to 40 feet (6-12.2 m) apart. One person runs back and forth between two people standing near the bases tossing the ball back and forth trying to tag the runner out before the runner arrives safely at either base. The game is lots of fun; keeps the runner working on back-and-forth movements, quickness, and deception; and can include practicing sliding into a base.

Pickle led to Brian's excitement about base stealing. He wanted to learn more because he found an area of the game in which he could have some success. Playing pickle early in his life did help him to become a good base stealer and eventually Major League Baseball's American League base-stealing champion in 2007.

I enjoy every opportunity to engage and challenge players to work on improving all areas of their baserunning and base stealing. When I work with players under the age of 12, it is relatively easy to prove to them in my teaching that speed is just a small element of success. I work with them to improve their running and comfort with variable leads and to be able to slide into a base with ease either feet first or head first.

I try to show athletes that a body's shape, whether perceived as good or bad, does not predetermine whether a player is quick or can maneuver the bases better than a teammate. I demonstrate to the athlete that technique and instincts often are more important in on-base situations than speed.

I usually can develop more confidence in younger players soon after I begin teaching them because fewer coaches have instilled in their players that only speed changes games on the bases. In many leagues for kids 12 and under, a player must keep his foot on the base until the ball is delivered, so players rarely try to steal. However, once baseball players have participated in a league for ages 13 and up, when many coaches constantly talk to only the speed guys about helping the team on the bases, I find a much larger challenge convincing athletes to accept that every team member has a chance to improve. Often, when I start teaching an average to below-average runner new to my philosophy that he can dramatically improve his baserunning skills, I have to spend a little more time and effort convincing him he can be more confident and successful at stealing bases.

Are coaches committing enough practice time for base stealing and baserunning? Do they separate base stealing from baserunning? Are they making practices "live" at times for game simulation? Are they taking video of practices so athletes can review their form, rhythm, and techniques?

DEVELOPING RUNNING FORM

A baseball player should become a track athlete in a baseball uniform. Improvement in an athlete's running form, regardless of speed, comes from enjoying running, running often, and being willing to work toward detailing the stride to perfection. In part IV, strength and conditioning for baseball are covered in more detail.

When I was growing up, I walked, ran, or biked just about everywhere I needed to go. My legs were in motion most of the day, which eventually helped my rhythm when running. Then, when I turned my runs into sprints, I had respectable form and decent speed. I became a better runner because I wanted to use my legs all day whether walking or running. Once again, this involved practice through repetition.

Today, many young people are a long way from using their legs all day. They use walking, biking, or running as a last resort if they cannot find a ride with four wheels attached. I would enjoy seeing more baseball athletes embrace running the way soccer players or cross-country runners do. However, this is not the norm for the current baseball world. Baseball players, of all athletes who participate in a sport requiring running, may be the least likely to work on their running form. Young baseball athletes seem to think that because the game requires only short bursts of speed they can somehow get by with minimal practice on their running skills.

Some baseball athletes are naturally blessed with respectable running form. But it is certainly a small percentage. Even a player who looks good running from home plate to first base after the ball is put in play does not necessarily run the bases well. Every athlete must practice good starts from a standstill position in an attempt to steal a base and work to improve his routes between bases as he attempts to take an extra base and score.

As mentioned, my son Brian has always liked to run the bases and ran reasonably well at a young age. However, he did not like to just go out and run unless it was in a baseball uniform. When he was a teenager I encouraged him to begin to work on and improve his form. Brian grew up near a college campus and knew there was an excellent track program at the university. When he was a junior in high school he stopped by the track office and asked if there was an assistant coach or former track athlete, maybe a graduate student, hanging around who would be willing to work with him.

The coaches did recommend a graduate student, Udah Shaw, who had some experience teaching running form and speed work and would work with him. This was definitely one of the best decisions Brian ever made to help his baseball career and to improve his ability to run the bases well. Coach Shaw was patient with the young athlete and taught him how to enjoy practicing running on his own. He gave him excellent fundamental teaching to improve his form and consistency of stride length and eventually helped him with speed work.

Are coaches providing all the resources possible for athletes to improve? Do athletes have one-on-one time with coaches if they show great interest? Do they work on running form as athletes do their warm-ups each day?

I encourage players to build the following routine to help improve their running form, which eventually should help their quickness and possibly their speed:

- Spend 10 to 15 minutes stretching the entire body each day.
- Learn proper alignment of the body for all exercises and proper form when running.
- Practice quick twitch drills and nerve activation movements daily.

- Find the correct exercises to increase the function of muscles used for running.
- Use equipment in practice that will improve stride consistency.
- Practice sprinting from a track start and a baseball start, which requires a crossover step.
- Review film of correct running form to retain a visual for help in making adjustments.
- Practice running form 4 to 6 days a week for 15 to 20 minutes.
- Practice 10 to 20 repetitions of 20- to 40-yard (or meter) sprints 4 to 6 days a week.
- If possible, find an experienced track coach to help with form and speed work.

Sliding ◇**2**◇

The art of sliding is extinct at practice. Coaches have pushed aside teaching the best slide for a given situation. Difficult to understand is why, since a great slide can be a game changer.

There is nothing more exciting than watching a polished slide into a base that avoids a tag, leaving the runner safe and the game altered or won. However, since athletes don't appreciate the importance of executing a slide, which slide to use in which situation, where to tag the base with a hand or foot, and how to move quickly to the next base after sliding on an overthrow, how can they be expected to make that game-changing slide?

Teach sliding on a slip and slide, which is a plastic sheathing 10 to 20 feet (3-6 m) wide by 20 to 50 feet (6.1-15 m) long, soaked with baby shampoo and kept wet with a running hose on the plastic. This allows players to slide easily on the surface. It's a safe and fun way to teach the various slides to all ages. Include lots of water and shampoo to make the plastic slick but safe. Athletes should wear helmets if running full speed from more than 30 feet (9 m).

Every Friday morning in my camps, which have athletes from 5 to 18 years of age, I set up a slip and slide. The campers slide for 60 to 90 minutes, getting lots of repetitions. It's hard to get them to quit the activity at the end of the morning session. They love it and want more time and opportunity.

Let's look at variations of the slide: bent leg, pop-up, hook, and head first.

BENT-LEG SLIDE

As a player prepares for a bent-leg slide (see figure 2.1), he should be running at full speed. The athlete wants to have early downward action in this slide to slightly slow momentum before either leg might touch the base. It helps at impact if the front or stiffer leg touches the base instead of going over it. The foot and ankle can handle the impact when a player is going full speed as long as the player slides early and not when almost at the base.

In the upper body, the first movement as the slide begins should be the hands reaching upward toward the sky. Sometimes players hit the ground with their hands because they have not practiced the correct arm action. When the hands stay down, they break the momentum of the slide, usually too much. This is poor mechanics. Sometimes wrist injuries occur due to a player putting his full body weight on the hands.

The runner's butt then sits square on the ground and directly at the bag. If an athlete turns his body to one side or the other and the butt is not flat on the ground, usually the slide slows him down too much, making it difficult to make both arms go skyward. Also, whichever side the athlete turns toward, that hand normally touches the ground to help break the momentum.

Figure 2.1 Bent-leg slide: *(a)* early downward action to slow momentum; *(b)* hands move up

Figure 2.1 *(continued)* *(c)* butt hits the ground directly at the bag; *(d)* top leg lined up with the bag, bottom leg folded under top leg; *(e)* straight leg skims over the bag; *(f)* player ends up lying over the base.

Each athlete should determine which leg is on top or bottom. The leg on top is usually lined up straight at the bag, at about 90 percent of extension, the heel near the ground and toes pointing at the sky. Some players will try to tip the toes down and catch the base, but this is very difficult to do and can lead to unnecessary injury. The bottom leg should be in an L shape folded under the straight leg. Many times when the athlete reaches base, the heel of the straight leg skims the top of the base, slides over the base, and the bent leg ends up butted up against the base.

As the athlete's butt hits the ground, the hands continue to go toward the sky and eventually end up over the head. The momentum of the arms going over the head normally carries the upper body backward until the entire body is lying flat on the ground, arms over the head. A few players just sit down and do not lie back, but this seems to be the slowest way to reach base using the bent-leg slide.

When learning the bent-leg slide, begin by running at half speed. Sit down easily and throw your hands toward the sky. This will help you learn to sit down softly. You can practice on grass, on a slip and slide, or indoors on blankets or cushioned pads.

The bent-leg slide is the most popular in baseball. A majority of players seem to feel comfortable using this slide. It provides them with less chance of injury, and athletes don't feel the need to practice the slide often to still execute it reasonably well.

The problem with the bent-leg slide is that players rarely show control of the top leg so the foot hits the bag immediately when it reaches the base. Due to the lack of control over where the front foot hits the bag, most of the time the extended leg passes over the bag without touching it and hangs in the air until the bent leg slides into the bag. This means the player has actually arrived at the base but not immediately touched it and may be tagged out after the straight leg passes over the bag but before the bent leg hits the base. If players worked on touching the base as softly as possible with the lead leg in a bent-leg slide, they would be safe more often.

To touch the base with the top leg during the bent-leg slide, the top leg must have some degree of flexibility to prevent injury. You can practice on a slip and slide outdoors or on blankets indoors. Run full speed, sit down, throw your hands toward the sky, and slide into the base, trying to touch the base with the top leg.

When the top leg slides over the bag during the bent-leg slide, the runner can still catch the bag with the bottom leg to stay safe. This too can be practiced on a slip and slide outdoors or on blankets inside. Again, run full speed, sit down, and throw your hands toward the sky. Slide into the base and try to touch the bag with your bottom leg as the top leg slides across the top of the base.

Bent-Leg Slide on Dirt, Grass, Slip and Slide, or Gymnasium Floor

OBJECTIVES

Learn to run at full speed. Slide as late as possible without landing on the base. Practice sitting on your butt with chest straight ahead. Throw hands skyward. Lie back; sometimes the lower back eventually touches the ground. Touch the front edge of the base softly with the foot of the straight leg or skim the top of the base as the foot of the straight leg slides across the base. Slide the bottom leg comfortably up against the base.

EQUIPMENT

No equipment is mandatory other than a safe area to slide. Having a base to slide into is helpful. If practicing on dirt or grass, it is best to slide into a base that moves or breaks away for safety. The slide can be practiced in dirt or on grass without a base. If using a base with the slip and slide, place the base at the edge of the grass so players will slide into the base as they exit the plastic surface. If using a gymnasium floor, thickly pile several blankets for players to practice sliding on. It is best for the athlete to wear a helmet whenever he practices sliding to help prevent head injuries.

EXECUTION

If there's more than one athlete, players form a line. One person completes the slide before the next player begins unless the drill is set up with two or three lines. The person at the head of the line sprints a minimum of 7 to 10 steps before sliding. Players start this drill from a stealing-lead or straight-ahead sprint position and run from as far away as 70 to 80 feet (21.3-24.4 m). Athletes sprint directly to the base and start the slide early enough to not go over the base except with the top leg.

COACHING POINTS

Athletes should run full speed and slide comfortably with rhythm. The hands should go to the sky as the butt hits the ground. Players should skim across the surface to the base.

Sliding Practice Guidelines

- Athletes should always practice with shoes off unless in a live drill with the team.

- When possible, practice outdoors on a slip and slide, water soaked and loaded with shampoo to make the surface slippery for good sliding. Athletes can wear pants or shorts.

- If practicing on Astroturf or field turf soaked with water, athletes should wear pants.

- If practicing on a grassy area, choose one that can be torn up. The surface can be wet or dry. Athletes should wear pants.

- Practice indoors on blankets or cushioned pads approximately 20 feet by 10 feet (6.1 m × 3 m). The blankets or pads should slide easily with body momentum on wood or another soft surface. Athletes can wear pants or shorts.

- Practice head-first and feet-first slides on a soft and smooth dirt surface. It is best to wear pants while practicing sliding to prevent leg burns, and always wear a helmet to help prevent head injuries.

BENT-LEG SLIDE TO THE SIDE OF THE BAG, TAGGING THE BASE WITH A HAND

Occasionally, a runner will use the bent-leg slide to go beside a base (see figure 2.2). An example is at home plate when the catcher has the plate blocked and the runner does not want to slam into his shin guards using a bent-leg slide. In this instance, the player slides on his butt beside or around the base using a bent-leg slide. Then he uses his hand to touch the base as he slides by it, if at home plate, or even goes all the way beyond the base and flips back over onto his stomach to reach for the base with his hand.

As a player prepares for a bent-leg slide to the side of the base, he should be running full speed. The athlete wants to have early downward action in this slide to slightly slow momentum before either leg might touch the base. In this slide, the early downward action is *not* as important as when using a bent-leg slide going straight into a base.

The hands are closer to the ground in this bent-leg slide to avoid a tag and give the player easier access to the bag. However, the hands should not be used to cushion the slide in order to maintain momentum. Also, the hand and wrist can be injured if the wrist takes too much weight or is stepped on by a defensive player.

When the slide begins, the runner's butt hits the ground. The runner is to the right or left side of the bag to prepare to avoid a defensive player waiting for the ball and blocking the base or already waiting for the runner with the baseball in his glove.

Each athlete should determine which leg is on top or bottom. The leg on top is usually at 90 percent extension, the heel near the ground and toes pointing at the sky. The bottom leg should be in an L shape folded under the straight leg.

Since the athlete is going beside the base, the slide occurs later than the bent-leg slide when the runner is going directly into a base. The runner wants to keep the acceleration going longer with this approach before hitting the dirt. The runner hits the dirt almost parallel to the base. He uses the left or right hand to grab the base very late and holds on or, if at home plate, swipes the base as the body is sliding past.

Figure 2.2 Bent-leg slide beside a base: *(a)* early downward action to slow momentum; *(b)* hands stay low; *(c)* butt hits the ground to the side of the bag; *(d)* player reaches with hand to touch base.

The runner may also decide to slide completely past the base if the defensive player is already holding the ball (see figure 2.3). In this instance, the runner flips his body over and uses the hand coming from the outside to reach out and grab the base.

Figure 2.3 Bent-leg slide past a base: *(a)* base runner begins bent-leg slide, defensive player is holding the ball; *(b)* base runner flips his body over and *(c)* uses the hand coming from the outside to touch the base.

Bent-Leg Slide to Avoid a Tag on Dirt, Grass, Slip and Slide, or Gymnasium Floor

OBJECTIVES

Learn to run full speed. Slide as late as possible to slide past the base. Practice sitting down on your butt with chest straight ahead. Keep hands in front of chest so hand can tag the bag easily.

EQUIPMENT

No equipment is mandatory other than a safe area to slide. Having a base to slide past is helpful. If practicing on dirt or grass, it is best to have a base securely in the ground to tag or grab. The slide can also be practiced in dirt or grass with an imaginary base. If using a base with the slip and slide, place the base at the edge of the plastic surface so players will slide to the side of the base as they exit the plastic surface. If using a gymnasium floor, thickly pile several blankets for players to practice sliding on. It is best to wear a helmet to prevent head injuries if running more than 30 feet (9.1 m) or running full speed.

EXECUTION

If there's more than one athlete, players form a line. One person completes the slide before the next player begins. If using two or three lines, more than one person can slide simultaneously. The person at the head of the line sprints a minimum of 7 to 10 steps before sliding. Players begin this drill from a starting position, such as a stealing-stance or straight-ahead sprint position, and run from as far away as 70 to 80 feet (21.3-24.4 m). The athlete sprints directly toward the base and begins to slide to one side or the other to practice using the right or left hand to either tag the base or grab the base to keep from going past. Normally players will use the side and hand that is most comfortable. This is not always the case, however. For example, if a runner is coming into second base and the throw is being made from right field, the player may slide to the third-base side of second base, which is usually the least favorite side for players to slide from.

COACHING POINTS

Athletes should run full speed and slide comfortably with rhythm. The hands should stay in front of the chest as the butt hits the ground. Players should skim a hand across the surface of the base if pretending the base is home plate or actually grab the base if pretending the base is first, second, or third.

POP-UP SLIDE

The pop-up slide (see figure 2.4) is an extension of the bent-leg slide. It is used when runners see an overthrow or the ball bounces away from the base or home plate area.

Figure 2.4   Pop-up slide: *(a)* bent-leg slide into base; *(b)* player pushes up from ground using hand; *(c)* player gets into upright position; *(d)* player advances.

The pop-up slide is the extension or completion of a bent-leg slide and helps a runner to pop up from the bent-leg sliding position in one fluid motion. The hands are held lower and, during the slide, may also be used to help push the body upright.

The pop-up slide is used when a runner sees an overthrow while running the bases or when the ball hits the runner going into the slide or hits the defensive player and bounces away. Sometimes the ball will skid under or through a defensive player late into a sliding play, and the runner uses the pop-up slide to quickly come up and advance. Finally, when a player sees or feels the catcher is not going to throw to the base when the player is going into the slide at second or third base, or the runner looks back at the plate and the ball has gotten away from the catcher, the runner uses the pop-up slide to have a better opportunity to advance.

In a pop-up slide, the player immediately starts back up to a running position as he makes contact with the ground. As a player prepares for a pop-up slide, he should be running full speed and sliding very late using the bent-leg slide. The athlete wants to stay upright as long as possible because the player is barely touching the ground before the legs, maybe with help from the hands, push the body back up from the base to the running position. In most instances the base is actually used to catapult the body upright. Usually the back is straight, as if the player were sitting in a chair, if the runner is anticipating popping up. The player goes down and up in one fluid motion and then looks to begin immediate movement toward the next base.

While learning the pop-up slide, it's best to practice on a slip and slide outdoors or blankets indoors. Run full speed. As you approach the base, barely sit down. As your body touches the ground, use the momentum of the slide and your hands, if necessary, to bring the body back up so you can possibly continue to run.

Pop-Up Slide on Dirt, Grass, Slip and Slide, or Gymnasium Floor

OBJECTIVES

Learn to run full speed. Slide as late as possible to pop up. Practice sitting down on your butt with chest straight ahead and back upright. Hands are kept low to possibly help catapult the body quickly up.

EQUIPMENT

No equipment is mandatory other than a safe area to slide. Having a base to slide into is helpful. If practicing with a base on dirt or grass, the base can be secured to the ground or laid loosely. The slide can be practiced in dirt or grass with an imaginary base. If using a base with the slip and slide, place the base on the grass at the edge of the plastic surface so players will slide to the base as they exit the plastic surface and push upward to pop up. It is best to wear a helmet if running more than 30 feet (9.1 m).

EXECUTION

If there's more than one athlete, players form a line. One person completes the slide before the next player begins. If using two or three lines, players can slide simultaneously. The person at the head of the line sprints a minimum of 7 to 10 steps before sliding. Players begin this drill from a stealing-stance or straight-ahead sprint position and run from as far away as 70 to 80 feet (21.3-24.4 m). The athlete sprints directly toward the base and begins to slide very late, barely touching the ground and popping up immediately.

COACHING POINTS

Athletes should run full speed and slide comfortably with rhythm in a bent-leg slide. The hands should stay in front of the chest as the butt hits the ground unless the player is using one hand to help him push off the ground. Players should barely touch the ground before pushing off the base to pop up quickly.

HOOK SLIDE

The hook slide was used often in the early 1900s and made famous by Ty Cobb, but it is almost extinct in today's game. Cobb was an aggressive base runner and was often looking to take the extra base. This created many close plays during which he used the hook slide to try to avoid the tag.

In today's game it is rare to see a player as aggressive as Cobb and as interested in consistently taking an extra base and possibly using a hook slide to avoid a tag. There does not seem to be a good theory or reason why the hook slide has almost become extinct in the game.

The idea of using a hook slide (see figure 2.5) comes from a runner reading a throw and realizing the play is going to be close at the base. He tries to see or anticipate as early as possible where the infielder sets up in accordance with a base and the angle at which the ball is thrown to the base. The runner then slides to the side of the base opposite the infielder. He catches the bag with the toes of the leg nearest the bag. This leg is dragging behind his upper body. He throws his front leg to the far outside of the base as if doing a split. The hand nearest the base grabs the bag if the foot happens to come off the base. This slide allows the runner to wait longer to hit the ground and gives the infielder less of the runner's body to tag.

Before sliding, the runner must read the infielder and know the angle at which the ball is thrown to the base. In the hook slide, the runner slides to the side of the base opposite that which the defensive player is setting up and usually waits very late to hit the ground. The runner sits down on his butt somewhat similar to the initiation of the bent-leg slide. However, as the body starts down, the lead leg kicks out away from the base. This lead-leg kickout usually happens at about the same time the defensive player is catching the ball or beginning the motion to tag the runner. As the lead leg kicks out, the upper body leans back and away from the fielder and the athlete drags the back leg to catch the toes of the dragging leg on the corner of the base. Dragging the leg on the side of the bag will slow the body down if a player slides extremely late. If the foot comes off the base, the hand nearest the base grabs the corner of the bag. When the slide is completed, the runner's legs are almost in a split position.

When first learning the hook slide, run at half speed. Get the feel of kicking the outside leg forward to place the body in a split position. You can practice on a slip and slide outdoors or on blankets indoors. Once you are comfortable at half speed, practice while running full speed. Practice kicking the outside leg forward to place the body in a split position. Practice catching the foot of the trailing leg on the corner of the base. The upper body leans back and away from the base as the back leg catches the base.

Figure 2.5 Hook slide: *(a)* Runner reads a close throw to the base; *(b)* he slides to the side of the bag opposite the infielder; *(c)* runner catches the bag with the toes of the leg nearest the bag.

Hook Slide on Dirt, Grass, Slip and Slide, or Gymnasium Floor

OBJECTIVES

Learn to run full speed. Slide as late as possible to the side of the base. Practice throwing the lead leg out in front of the body and dragging the other leg behind the body. This places you in a split-leg position at the end of the slide. The upper body leans back and the hands go above the head. Sometimes the upper body stays almost upright, but in other hook slides the back is almost flat on the ground depending on how much the runner needs to avoid the tag.

EQUIPMENT

No equipment is mandatory other than a safe area to slide. Having a base to slide into is helpful with the hook slide so the athlete can grab the bag if the foot comes off at the end of the slide. If practicing on dirt or grass, the base can be secured to the ground or laid loosely. The slide can be practiced in dirt or grass with an imaginary base. If using a base with the slip and slide, place the base on the far end of the plastic surface so players will slide to the side of the base as they exit the plastic surface. It is best to wear a helmet when practicing sliding.

EXECUTION

If there's more than one athlete, players form a line. One person completes the slide before the next player begins unless the drill is set up with two or three lines. The person at the head of the line sprints a minimum of 7 steps before sliding. Players begin this drill from a stealing-stance or straight-ahead sprint position and run from as far away as 80 feet (~24 m). The athlete sprints directly toward the base and begins to slide very late to one side of the base. To make the drill more realistic and challenging, consider adding a defensive player.

COACHING POINTS

Athletes should run full speed and learn to kick the lead leg out in front of the body. The back leg drags to slow the body down and the foot catches the corner of the base. The hand nearest the base is the safety if the foot comes off the base. The player practices a split-leg position as he slides. The upper body should lean back toward the ground and away from the defensive player to avoid a tag.

HEAD-FIRST SLIDE

The head-first slide is the fastest and most efficient way to reach a base. However, I teach runners to never use the head-first slide when going into home plate unless they are sliding around the plate to come in from the back side.

The head-first slide is exciting to learn. Runners can stay full speed as they hit the ground and learn to attack the base instead of throttling down as they approach. As runners begin the slide, they should imagine actually flying close to the ground. An efficient head-first slide is explosive.

When the runner leaves his feet he is flying low and parallel to the ground (see figure 2.6). As the runner approaches the base at full speed, he leans forward and then throws his hands out in front as if the hands are trying to cross the finish line of a sprint before the rest of the body.

Figure 2.6 For the head-first slide, the runner flies low and parallel to ground, hands out in front.

When learning the head-first slide, the runner should measure the length of the slide once the chest hits the surface. This aids in understanding the importance of momentum in traveling to the base. Runs are at full speed with extended arms. A coach should measure the distance of the slide once the chest hits the surface. For younger players, it's best to practice on a wet plastic surface such as a water slide outdoors, or indoors on a hardwood floor covered with blankets or cushioned pads.

Base runners should throw the hands and arms out in front of the body as if they are trying to fly low to the ground whether going straight into a base or to the side of a base. The body should be level with the ground.

When sliding head first, there are several ways to approach the base:

• Sliding to the side of the base (see figure 2.7*a*). Possibly used when the runner is stealing a base and knows the ball and infielder will all arrive at approximately the same time. The runner wants to avoid a collision with the infielder by going to the appropriate side of the base.

• Sliding directly into the base (see figure 2.7*b*). Used only when the base is clear of any obstruction and there is little concern that the runner's arms and upper body will collide with the defensive player's legs before the runner gets to the base. Also, the slide should begin very early so the runner does not go over the base with his upper body.

• Sliding into home plate if the pitcher or corner infielder is making the tag (see figure 2.7*c*). I encourage players to never go head first into home plate if the catcher is making the tag. The runner can be more open to using the head-first slide when a player not wearing the catcher's gear is making the play. This is similar to sliding head first into second or third base.

• Sliding into first base (see figure 2.7*d*). For some plays at first base, the runner has to make a last-second decision on whether to slide. The runner sees midway down the line that the first baseman is changing his feet to move toward a poor throw or the pitcher is covering and the runner would like to avoid a full-body collision. These occasions are rare. If the runner does slide, it should be to the dugout side of the base and the left hand should drag across the base as the runner slides past. Because this is a reaction play, it is best not to practice it.

Figure 2.7 Head-first slide situations: *(a)* slide to the side of the base; *(b)* slide directly into the base; *(c)* slide into home plate when the pitcher or corner infielder is making the tag; *(d)* slide into first base.

Head-First Slide on Slip and Slide

OBJECTIVES

Learn to run full speed and then slide to and touch a specific part of the base.

EQUIPMENT

You need a safe area to slide and a plastic sheet when making a slide. Although this drill is best practiced on a plastic slide with shampoo and water, it can work to practice on grass, dirt, or blankets on a gymnasium floor. If using a base with the water slide, place the base on the far end of the plastic surface so players will slide to the base as they exit the plastic surface. It is best to wear a helmet when practicing sliding.

EXECUTION

If there's more than one athlete, players form a line. One person completes the slide before the next player begins unless the drill is set up with two or three lines. The person at the head of the line sprints a minimum of 7 steps before sliding. Players begin this drill from a stealing-stance or straight-ahead sprint position and run from as far away as 80 feet (about 24 m). The athlete sprints directly toward the base and begins to slide very early, extending the hands first and then laying the body out parallel to the ground.

COACHING POINTS

Athletes should run full speed and concentrate on throwing their hands out in front of the body early, which helps prevent shoulder injuries when using the head-first slide. The runner does not jump into the slide but gradually lowers the body and skims across the surface with his chest and does not bounce into the air when he hits the surface. The athlete keeps his head up so his eyes can see exactly where the hand should touch the base.

◇—◇—◇

Head-First Slide Directly to the Front of the Base

The runner slides very early so his hands barely touch the base. Body momentum is stopped right at the edge of the base (see figure 2.8). The arms are fully extended out in front, and the hands reach for the base. The chest barely hits the ground so there is little friction to slow down the body early in the slide. The head should be up, looking straight ahead so the eyes can see the area of the bag the hands should touch. The runner's momentum should stop before the upper body hits the base.

Figure 2.8   *(a)* On a head-first slide directly to the front of the base, *(b)* the body's momentum stops at the edge of the base before the upper body goes over.

Practice the head-first slide directly into the base on a slip and slide, blankets, a padded mat, or a soft dirt surface. Run at full speed. Fully extend your arms and slide very early. Use trial and error to discover how far away from the base your body needs to hit the ground so it stops before going over the base.

Head-First Slide to the Side of the Base

On a head-first slide to the side of the base, the runner slides very late to the side of the base most open from the play the defense is trying to make. Most head-first slides to the side of the base are to the outfield side of second or third base. As the runner slides to the outfield side of the base, the left hand catches the corner of the base and the right arm extends straight in front. The palms of the hands take a lot of the force of the slide, which keeps the core of the body just barely touching the surface to maintain speed instead of the ground slowing down the body. The head should be up and eyes forward to see the hand touch the corner of the base. The runner's full body should slide past the base, and the hand should slide across the top edge of the base (see figure 2.9a). If the hand comes off the far side of the base, the left foot should make contact and hook the corner of the base so the body is always in contact with the bag (figure 2.9b). Athletes should practice this slide often, working on catching the base with the hand or foot so the runner does not lose a stolen base due to totally exiting the base.

Figure 2.9   (a) On a head-first slide to the side of the base, the runner's body slides past the base and his hands slide across the top. (b) If the left hand comes off the base, the base runner catches the corner of the base to keep the body in contact with the bag.

When learning the head-first slide to the side of the base, run full speed and slide to the side of the base with the inside arm extended. Learn to touch and hold on to the inside corner of the base.

Because sometimes the hand slides over the base, you also need to learn to catch the base with your foot when making a head-first slide into the base. Run full speed and slide to the side of the base very late. Touch the inside corner of the base with the hand but continue to slide off the base. Catch the inside corner of the base with the back foot.

Experienced players can practice these slides on dirt. A slip and slide outdoors or blankets on a gymnasium floor provide the opportunity for more repetitions.

Head-First Slide to the Side of the Base on a Slip and Slide

OBJECTIVES

Learn to run full speed and to slide to and touch the outfield corner of the base.

EQUIPMENT

You need a base, a safe area to slide, and a plastic sheet if making a slip and slide. Although it is best to practice this slide on a slip and slide, you can practice on grass, dirt, or blankets on a gymnasium floor. If using a base with the slip and slide, place the base on the far end of the plastic surface so players will slide to the base as they exit the plastic surface. It is best to wear a helmet when practicing sliding.

EXECUTION

If there's more than one athlete, players form a line. One person completes the slide before the next player begins unless the drill is set up with two or three lines. The person at the head of the line sprints a minimum of 7 to 10 steps before sliding. Players can begin this drill from a stealing-stance or straight-ahead sprint position and run from as far away as 70 to 80 feet (21.3-24.4 m). The athlete sprints to the outside of the base and begins to slide very early, extending the hands first and then laying the body out parallel to the ground. The hand touches the outfield corner of the base.

COACHING POINTS

Athletes should run full speed and concentrate on throwing their hands out in front of the body early, which helps to prevent shoulder injuries when using the head-first slide. The runner skims across the surface with his chest and does not bounce into the air when he hits the surface. The athlete keeps his head up so he can see exactly where the hand should touch the base. If the athlete slides late and his hand goes across the top of the base, he catches the corner of the base with the inside of his foot as the hand comes off.

Leading Off ◆3◆

Before a player learns how to lead off from a base, he must understand the responsibilities of a base runner once he arrives at a base. While the runner is standing on the base he should go through a clear-cut routine.

The runner should look to see where the pitcher is located and never leave a base until he knows specifically where the ball is located. This is to protect against the hidden ball trick. Is the pitcher on the grassy part of the infield or the dirt portion of the mound? If on the dirt portion of the mound, the pitcher must have the baseball. If the pitcher does not have the baseball and is standing on the dirt portion of the mound, it is considered a balk. If the pitcher is on the grassy area of the infield, then the ball can be anywhere on the field and a runner can be tagged out if he steps off the base.

The runner should always check the positioning of the infielders and outfielders before leaving a base. He then should pick up the coach giving the signals. Also, the runner should know the distance to the cut of the grass to help him determine his lead while his eyes are directed at the pitcher and possibly glancing at the catcher as well.

UNDERSTANDING LEADS

A player should work hard to understand the best footage for him and what each part of his body is doing when taking a primary (or comfort zone), variable (or stealing), or secondary lead.

Primary, or Comfort Zone, Lead

Most coaches refer to the first steps a base runner takes from a base to the distance where he stops as a primary lead. This term still fits today if the athlete is repeating the same lead from each base, using a similar distance and the same footwork to attain that distance. However, if the primary lead is the final distance covered, then the runner is taking a moneyball philosophy to leads. This philosophy means the runner takes smaller leads and is rarely going to steal a base, so lead size means little, and the variations and threat of a quality lead are minimal.

I use the term *primary lead* (see figure 3.1) when teaching the first principle of leads: Runners should learn their comfort zone immediately after leaving any base. The comfort zone lead is a primary, or short, lead that allows the base runner to fall back to the base and touch it if a pickoff attempt is made. Once a runner is past the distance, which is equal to his height except when at second base, he is moving from a primary lead to a variable or stealing lead.

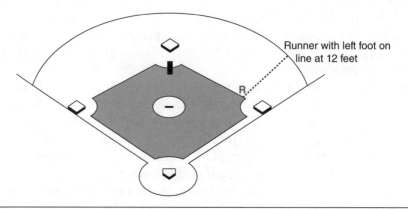

Figure 3.1 Primary, or comfort zone, lead.

Primary, or Comfort Zone, Lead

OBJECTIVES

The base runner learns to use his feet the same way each time he takes a primary (comfort zone) lead. The runner should feel as comfortable off the base as he does standing on it. The runner practices a relaxed athletic stance and learns to move in both directions with ease.

EQUIPMENT

Leads can be practiced almost anywhere. The best area is on a regulation field. You will need a base or can draw a line on the ground or place a chalk mark on a gymnasium floor.

EXECUTION

Draw lines 6, 7, and 8 feet (1.8, 2.1, 2.4 m) from the base. The runner repeats his first couple of steps until he knows how to reach one of these lines with his left foot consistently, even with his eyes closed. This gives the runner a good basic lead to begin from in most situations. If several runners want to practice, draw an extended line at those distances and line up bases so all runners can work at the same time.

COACHING POINTS

The athlete should always be natural and comfortable in his movements as he leaves a base. The runner should learn to be consistent with his feet as he takes a primary lead.

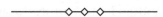

Variable Lead

I use the term *variable lead* to encourage athletes to be more knowledgeable about and learn flexibility with their lead footage. The footage can vary from 3 to 12 feet (1-3.7 m) at first and third base and from 8 to 24 feet (2.4-7.3 m) at second base.

Footwork style depends on what the runner is comfortable using. Once the runner arrives at the minimum footage from any base, he then must work on one of three styles of footwork, which are discussed in more detail in the chapters on base stealing: a slide step with the right foot out, followed by the left foot sliding back under the hip; a walking lead, in which the athlete takes a very short lead and uses creeping-like steps toward the next base; and the controlled jump lead at first base or the explosive jump lead at second base. The jump lead is rarely if ever used at third base. The variable lead helps the runner to be more aggressive in his leads and anticipatory in his jumps.

When using variable leads, a standard primary lead is totally discarded. The runner is not taking a set lead and then adjusting. Depending on the base and situation, the lead may be extremely small (mostly used as a decoy) or larger and more daring (see figure 3.2).

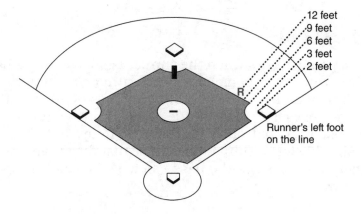

Figure 3.2 Variable lead.

Variable Lead

OBJECTIVES

The base runner learns to use his feet the same way each time he takes a variable lead. The runner should feel as comfortable off the base as he does standing on it. The runner practices a relaxed athletic stance and learns to move in both directions with ease.

EQUIPMENT

Leads can be practiced almost anywhere. The best area is a regulation field in the first-base area. Use a base or draw a line on the ground or a chalk mark on a gymnasium floor.

EXECUTION

Draw a line at 3, 6, 9, and 12 feet (1, 1.8, 2.7, and 3.7 m). The runner repeats his first couple of steps until he knows how to reach each line with his left foot consistently, even with his eyes closed. This gives the runner several variable leads to begin from in most situations. If several runners want to practice, draw an extended line at those distances and line up bases so all runners can work simultaneously.

COACHING POINTS

The athlete should always be natural and comfortable in his movements as he leaves a base. The runner should be consistent with his feet as he takes a variable lead and learns to move easily in both directions.

Secondary Lead

A secondary lead occurs when the runner is not stealing a base and the pitch is thrown to home plate. The runner has taken either a primary or variable lead, is not running or has stopped his attempted run, and then uses his feet to shuffle, chest facing home plate, toward the next base in a controlled manner (see figure 3.3). The secondary lead should stop within a reasonable distance from the base so the runner can return to the base safely if the catcher attempts a pickoff throw.

Figure 3.3 Runner at first taking a secondary lead toward second.

Secondary Lead

OBJECTIVES

The base runner learns to shuffle his feet the same way each time he takes a secondary lead, regardless of which base he is on. The runner should feel extremely comfortable with additional shuffles as he lengthens the lead with a secondary bounce as the pitch is delivered to home plate. The runner should be relaxed at the new distance from the base and learn to move in both directions with ease.

EQUIPMENT

Leads can be practiced almost anywhere. The best area is a regulation field near each of the bases. Draw a line on the ground or a chalk mark on a gymnasium floor to simulate the distance the player would shuffle off the base.

EXECUTION

The base runner takes his initial lead. Distance can vary. As the pitch is thrown to the plate, the runner shuffles the feet to a comfortable distance from the base where he can safely move in either direction.

(continued)

(continued)

COACHING POINTS

The athlete should always be natural and comfortable in his movements as he leaves a base and shuffles farther from the base. Rhythm with the shuffle steps allows good balance and the runner to move in both directions easily.

LEADS FROM FIRST BASE

Once the batter reaches first base, he is responsible for advancing. The next batter should help with that, too, but there is a lot the base runner can do to advance himself along the basepaths without the benefit of a hit or sacrifice fly.

Primary Lead From First Base

The distance of the primary lead is the same at first and third base. This primary-lead distance doubles at second base.

To find the distance of the primary lead during practice, the runner draws lines in the dirt at approximately 6, 7, and 8 feet (1.8, 2.1, and 2.4 m). If several athletes are working on primary leads at the same time, draw a long line toward right field so each runner has a line on which to place the left foot. Athletes leave the base with similar footwork each time to reach this distance.

The head is always up with the eyes in the direction of the pitcher (see figure 3.4). However, a runner may learn to look out of the corner of the right eye at the pitcher when leading off at first base and look at signals the catcher is giving at the same time. This helps the runner know when to run and be more successful.

It is good to practice taking leads with the eyes closed. This helps the runner learn more about how the lower half of the body works and how to take a similar lead each time. Repetitive practicing of similar footwork makes a runner more comfortable with all kinds of leads.

Footage can be anywhere from 8 to 12 feet (2.4-3.7 m), with a majority of runners setting up in the 9- to 11-foot (2.7-3.4 m) space off the base. The base runner should leave the base in an athletic position, which means knees flexed, feet never more than 18 inches (45.7 cm) apart at any time, and chest cupped over slightly (see figure 3.5). The feet should be kept directly under the hips. From 3 to 6 feet (1-1.8 m), the initial part of the lead, the athlete should move the feet in a comfortable and easily repeatable way each time he returns to first base. Consistency with the feet is extremely important with leads at any base.

Figure 3.4 Base runner taking a primary lead at first base, head up and eyes on the pitcher.

Figure 3.5 Athletic position during the primary lead from first base: knees flexed, feet about 18 inches (30 cm) apart and directly under the hips, chest cupped over slightly.

Once the feet leave the base, the head should always be looking at the pitcher. However, as a runner becomes more experienced, the eyes or peripheral vision can see both the pitcher and catcher, so a runner might have an indication of what pitch is being called without moving the head.

The second part of the primary lead should be taken with the right foot always leading the footwork. This way the right foot can be planted quickly to push off and return to first base safely if the pitcher decides to throw over during a runner's movement. The right foot moves approximately 6 to 8 inches (15-20 cm) toward second base, and the left foot pulls back up under the body so the runner remains in an athletic stance with the feet under the hips. The runner can then settle in for a comfortable primary lead, which is usually from 9 to 11 feet (2.7-3.4 m).

When a runner has completed the primary lead, his feet should be pointed straight ahead. On a few exceptions, athletes turn the lead, or right, foot open toward second base, but this can cause struggles when players need to return to first base quickly.

Footwork is critical to improving as a base stealer. When the runner returns to the base (see figure 3.6), the left foot should turn just slightly. The toes stay closed, which locks in the foot for strength on the turn, and the right foot crosses over with a long initial step toward the base.

Figure 3.6 Returning to first base from the primary lead: *(a)* Left foot turns slightly and toes stay closed to lock the foot as the base runner turns; *(b)* the right foot crosses over in a long step back toward first base.

Footwork when the runner is taking off for the next base (see figure 3.7) works the same as when returning to the base. The right foot should turn just slightly, and the toes stay closed to lock in the foot for strength on the turn. The left foot crosses over with a long initial step toward the next base.

Figure 3.7 Taking off for second base: *(a)* Right foot turns slightly and toes stay closed to lock the foot as the base runner turns; *(b)* the left foot crosses over in a long step toward second base.

A base runner's arms should be relaxed at his sides. Movement by both arms should be in sync and complementary. The lead-arm side, or the side toward which the runner is turning, should pull into the hip area. The offside arm thrusts out and slightly upward toward the base to which the runner is moving.

Eyes-Closed Lead

OBJECTIVES

Learn to synchronize the movement of the body while taking a primary lead from first base. Develop the ability to visualize taking a proper primary lead while coordinating the body to move athletically and consistently.

EQUIPMENT

A baseball field with a marker placed 12 feet (3.7 m) from first base.

(continued)

(continued)

EXECUTION

The base runner stands on first base and closes his eyes. He should see no daylight with his eyes closed. The head is up and the chin level so the eyes are still directed at the pitcher's mound. His first two steps can be side-by-side or even crossover steps since the runner is still close enough to the base that he could actually fall onto it if there is a pickoff attempt. The steps do not have to be done with as much precision to attain a 6-foot (1.8 m) lead with the left foot. Once the runner is standing at 6 feet with the left foot, he must learn the most efficient way to attain a 12-foot (3.7 m) lead, finishing with his left foot on or near the marker. He must learn to consistently, efficiently, and sometimes quickly make this footage.

COACHING POINTS

Often athletes cannot or do not visualize what each foot is doing, what their arms and hands are doing, and if they are taking the lead athletically so they can move well to the left or right. Each runner should learn more about how to make his body parts move in union when he leaves the base. Athletes learn this much faster through eyes-closed drills.

A majority of runners have the same basic movement after they reach 6 feet (1.8 m) with the left foot. The right foot reaches out approximately 8 to 12 inches (20.3-30.5 cm), and the left foot pulls up under the hip to place the runner in an athletic position. The head is always up and looking at the pitcher even with the eyes closed. Tall and very long-legged athletes usually gain even more ground than a maximum of 12 inches and still keep their feet less than 18 inches (~45 cm) apart. This keeps them in an athletic position from which movement to the left or right is still quick and easy.

Most athletes end up at or near the 12-foot (3.7 m) marker with the left foot by taking either two or three right- to left-foot steps. Some runners take a controlled hop after the first or second movement with the right foot to reach the 12-foot marker. This hop, still keeping the feet underneath the athlete, allows the runner to reach the 12-foot marker quicker.

It will take the athlete many repetitions with his eyes closed to find the best footwork to use from the time he leaves the base until he nears the 12-foot marker. Repetition is a must in this drill to develop consistent footwork.

The runner will learn how to place the left foot on or near the same marker each time he takes a primary or comfort zone lead. The athlete now has a primary lead to work from each time on base, no matter the situation or caliber of the pitcher's pickoff move. This is a safe, comfortable, nonstealing lead.

Variable Lead From First Base

The distance of the variable lead is the same at first and third base. This variable-lead distance doubles at second base.

During practice, the runner draws a line in the dirt at 3, 6, 9, and 12 feet (1, 1.8, 2.7, and 3.7 m). If several athletes are practicing at the same time, the line is drawn longer toward right field in the first-base area so each athlete has a line on which to place his left foot. Athletes leave the base using similar footwork each time, no matter the distance of the lead.

The head is always up and eyes in the direction of the pitcher. However, a runner may learn to look out of the corner of the right eye at the pitcher when leading off at first base and look at signals the catcher is giving at the same time. This helps the runner know when to run and allows more success.

The athlete should practice with his eyes closed to push the mind and body to learn how the feet attain each footage marker. The player should keep his head up even though the eyes are closed for practice. He opens his eyes after each attempt to hit a footage marker with the left foot.

Repetition is so important in improving all aspects of taking leads at each footage marker. The runner should use similar footwork to attain each footage marker. Many repetitions are required to make this occur easily.

The athlete learns to use variable leads through this process. Variable leads make it difficult for the opposing pitcher, coach, and team to pick up on when the runner may or may not attempt to steal. Each lead, even the shortest, can turn into a stealing lead. Some leads act as a primary lead, allowing the runner to turn the footage into a secondary lead.

Lead footage can be anywhere from 1 to 12 feet (0.3-3.7 m), with a runner potentially using different footage each time on the base or even for each pitch. This gives the base runner a distinct mental and possible physical advantage over the pitcher and defense. The defense is guessing whether the runner knows what he is doing and whether or not he will run from a shorter lead. Some runners use a walking lead when varying their leads, which helps them get a good jump when running. A few use the jump lead, which I teach and learned from my son Brian Roberts, who is the only major league player currently using a jump lead at first base with a variable lead.

The base runner should leave the base in an athletic position, which means knees flexed, feet never more than 18 inches (45.7 cm) apart at any time, and chest cupped over slightly. The feet should be kept directly under the hips. From 3 to 6 feet (1-1.8 m), the initial part of the lead, the athlete should move the feet in a comfortable and easily repeatable way each time he returns to first base. Consistency with the feet is extremely important with leads at any base.

Once the feet leave the base, the head should always be looking at the pitcher. However, as a runner becomes more experienced, the eyes or peripheral vision can see both the pitcher and catcher so a runner might have an indication of what pitch is being called without moving the head.

The footwork for the variable lead should be taken with the right foot always leading. This way the right foot can be planted quickly to push off and return to the base safely if the pitcher decides to throw over during a runner's movement. The right foot moves approximately 6 to 8 inches (15-20 cm) toward second base, and the left foot pulls back up under the body so the runner continues in an athletic stance with the feet under the hips. The runner can then settle in for a comfortable variable lead and use a different footage for each pitch or each time on first base.

When a runner has completed his variable lead, his feet should be pointed straight ahead (see figure 3.8). On a few exceptions, athletes turn the lead, or right, foot open toward second base, but this can cause struggles when players need to return to the base quickly.

Secondary Lead at First Base

After leaving first base, the base runner can take any primary or variable lead and turn it into a secondary lead once the pitch is delivered to home plate. The feet may be stationary or slowly moving, depending on the game situation and the base the runner is on.

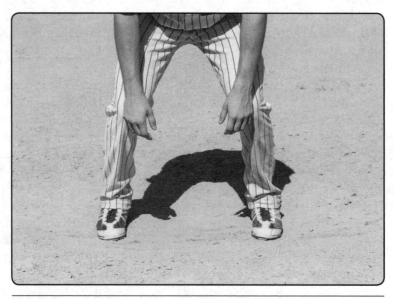

Figure 3.8 At the completion of the variable lead from first base, the runner's feet point straight ahead.

When the pitch is delivered to home plate, the runner uses a shuffling footwork to move toward the next base in a controlled manner (see figure 3.9). It is important the athlete know the catcher's arm strength and the positioning of the infielders so he does not move too far off the base and can get back safely if there is a pickoff throw.

Figure 3.9 The base runner shuffles his feet in the secondary lead from first base when the pitch is delivered to home plate.

The secondary lead from first base is the completion of a primary or variable lead when the runner is not attempting to steal a base. As the pitch is in the process of being thrown to the plate, the runner continues with the same mechanics used when taking the primary or variable lead. Wherever the runner happens to be with his lead foot when the pitcher makes a move toward home plate, the right foot takes a 6- to 8-inch (15-20 cm) shuffle step (the shuffle steps keep the runner under control with his chest and feet facing straight ahead), and the left foot is pulled under the body so both feet continue to stay under the hips. The runner can take several shuffle steps to extend his lead. The number of steps varies depending on the game situation and how comfortable a secondary lead the runner can safely take without concern of being picked off by the catcher if the ball is not hit.

LEADS FROM SECOND BASE

Second base presents new challenges to the base runner. He has to contend with two infielders, the shortstop and second baseman, he doesn't have a coach right there to help him assess the situation, and he is in scoring position. How he takes his lead at second can help determine if he will be able to move into third or even score, whether on a hit, sacrifice, or steal.

Primary Lead From Second Base

The primary lead at second base is taken with the feet directly in line between second and third base. Distance can be anywhere from 14 to 18 feet (4.3-5.5 m); a majority of runners set up in the 15- to 17-foot (4.6-5.2 m) space off second base. The base runner should leave the base in an athletic position, with the feet directly under the hips. Since a defensive player does not stand at the base to hold the runner on, the runner can take a more leisurely lead than at first base. However, the runner should definitely know his distance from the base at all times, just like at first base. The athlete should move the feet in a comfortable and easily repeatable way each time he returns to base. Consistency with the feet is extremely important with leads at any base.

Once the feet leave the base, the head should always be looking at the pitcher. At second base the runner has a direct view of the pitcher and catcher, which can help the runner pick up what pitch is being thrown. This can help make the runner's decision on whether to attempt to steal third base on, for example, a curve ball versus a fastball. More experience in picking up pitches can certainly be a big help in successful stealing, but the key is always beautiful rhythm, footwork, and timing by the base stealer.

The second phase of the primary lead at second base should be taken with the right foot always leading the footwork. This way the right foot can be planted quickly to push off and return to the base safely if the pitcher decides to throw over during a runner's movement. The right foot moves approximately 6 to 8 inches (15-20 cm) toward second base, and the left foot pulls back up under the body so the runner continues in an athletic stance with the feet under the hips (see figure 3.10). The runner can then settle in for a comfortable primary lead, usually from 17 to 20 feet (5.2-6 m).

Figure 3.10   The base runner takes his primary lead off second base, bringing his feet under his hips and maintaining an athletic stance.

When a runner completes the primary lead, his feet should be pointed straight ahead. On a few exceptions, athletes turn the lead, or right, foot open toward third base, but this can cause struggles when players need to return to the base quickly.

Footwork is critical to improving as a base stealer. When the runner returns to second base, the left foot turns just slightly, the toes stay closed to lock in the foot for strength on the turn, and the right foot crosses over with a long initial step back toward second base. Footwork when the runner is taking off for third base works the same way.

A base runner's arms should be relaxed and to his sides. Movement by both arms should be in sync and athletic. The lead arm, on the side toward which the runner is turning, pulls into the hip. The offside arm thrusts out and slightly upward toward the base to which the runner is moving.

Nonstealing Primary Lead at Second Base

Many coaches teach a nonstealing primary lead at second base. This lead begins with the runner taking the initial three to four steps, which is approximately 10 to 12 feet (3-3.7 m), at a 45-degree angle toward the shortstop hole and then turning the right hip back to where the body is once again facing straight toward the pitcher's mound (see figure 3.11). The remaining part of the lead is taken angularly toward third base so the runner can make an excellent

Figure 3.11 Nonstealing primary lead from second base: *(a)* Runner's initial steps are taken at a 45-degree angle toward the shortstop hole; *(b)* at around 10 to 12 feet (3-3.7 m), the runner turns the right hip so the body is facing straight toward the pitcher's mound.

turn at third base if the ball leaves the infield area as a hit. All the concepts for the lead are the same as those for the primary lead taken directly at the base, and the distances are approximately the same.

It's possible for a runner to steal third base after taking a non-stealing lead that takes him much deeper from the primary running path. The runner does this by gradually creeping back closer to the direct baseline as he increases his primary lead.

Variable Lead From Second Base

Variable is such a perfect word to use at second base because a base runner can adjust his distances and angles in so many ways. A runner can take multiple distances since no defensive player is at the base. This makes it difficult to give examples of the best ways to take variable leads at second base. Each athlete will probably use a different variable-lead approach.

Footage can be anywhere from 8 to 24 feet (2.4-7.3 m), with a runner possibly using different footage each time on second base or even for each pitch. This gives the base runner a distinct mental and possible physical advantage over the pitcher and defense. The defense has to guess if the runner knows what he is doing and whether or not he will run from a short or long lead. The key with variable leads at second base is the decoy movement the runner uses with his left shoulder and left foot.

For the variable lead, some runners use a walking or jump lead, which helps them gain an explosive start when running. Brian Roberts has one of the highest base-stealing percentages stealing third in the history of baseball, and he uses variable distances and jump leads more than anyone in the major leagues.

The base runner should leave second base in an athletic position, with the feet directly under the hips. From 3 to approximately 16 feet (1-4.9 m), the initial part of the lead, the athlete should move the feet in a comfortable and easily repeatable way each time he returns to second base.

Once the feet leave the base, the head should always be looking at the pitcher. At second base the runner can see both the pitcher and catcher, so a runner might have an indication of what pitch is being called. This will help him know the best pitch to run on. With experience, this becomes a key ingredient to a high-percentage success rate stealing third base.

The footwork for the variable lead should be taken with the right foot always leading. This way the right foot can be planted quickly to push off and return to the base safely if the pitcher decides to throw over during a runner's movement. The right foot moves approximately 6 to 8 inches (15-20 cm) toward third base, and the left foot pulls back up under the body so the runner continues in an athletic stance with the feet under the hips. The runner can then settle in for a comfortable variable lead at a different footage for each pitch or each time on second base.

When a runner has completed the variable lead, his feet should be pointed straight ahead. On a few exceptions, athletes turn the lead, or right, foot open toward third base, but this can cause struggles when players need to move quickly in either direction.

Secondary Lead at Second Base

For the secondary lead at second base, double the distance of the secondary lead at first and third base.

The secondary lead is the completion of a primary or variable lead when the runner is not attempting to steal third base. As the pitch is made to the plate, the runner continues with the same mechanics introduced earlier in taking a primary or variable lead. Wherever the runner happens to be with his lead when the pitcher makes a move toward home plate, the right foot takes a 6- to 8-inch (15-20 cm) shuffle step, chest and feet straight ahead, and the left foot is pulled under the body so both feet continue to stay under the hips. The runner can take several shuffle steps to extend the lead. The number of steps varies depending on the game situation and how comfortable a secondary lead the runner can safely take without the concern of being picked off by the catcher if the ball is not hit.

LEADS FROM THIRD BASE

The base runner is almost home. He can now score easily on a hit or sacrifice or, possibly, on a steal of home. Although it's important to be aggressive on the basepaths, the base runner should keep in mind the game situation. No runner wants to make the third out of the inning at third base.

Primary Lead From Third Base

Footage can be anywhere from 8 to 12 feet (2.4-3.7 m), with a majority of runners setting up in the 9- to 11-foot (2.7-3.4 m) space off third base. Whether the pitcher is right- or left-handed doesn't matter at third. The lead should be taken very comfortably and be easily repeatable each time the athlete returns to third base.

Once the feet leave the base, the head should always be looking at the pitcher. The runner's peripheral vision should pick up the third baseman if he changes how close he is playing to the base.

The second part of the primary lead should be taken with the right foot leading. This way the right foot can be planted quickly to push off and return to third base safely if the pitcher decides to throw over during a runner's movement. The right foot moves approximately 6 to 8 inches (15-20 cm) toward home plate, and the left foot pulls back up under the body so the runner continues in an athletic stance with the feet under the hips. The runner can then settle in for a comfortable primary lead versus a right- or left-handed pitcher.

When a runner completes the primary lead, his feet should be pointed straight ahead. On a few exceptions, athletes turn the lead, or right, foot open toward home plate, but this can cause struggles when players need to return to the base quickly.

Footwork is critical to improving as a base runner. When the runner returns to the base, the left foot should turn just slightly, and the toes stay closed to lock in the foot for strength on the turn. The right foot crosses over with a long initial step toward the base.

Footwork when the runner is taking off for home works the same as when returning to the base. The right foot turns just slightly. The toes stay closed to lock in the foot for strength on the turn. The left foot crosses over with a long initial step toward the next base.

A base runner's arms stay relaxed and to his sides. Movement by both arms should be in sync and athletic. Although runners rarely steal home, and so don't need the explosive movement when turning to the right like they do at first and second base, they often must react quickly to plays. This could lead to the runner needing an explosive turn to the right for a sprint toward home plate.

Variable Lead From Third Base

Lead length at third base is usually determined by how close the third baseman is playing to the base and whether the pitcher is left- or right-handed. When the third baseman is playing even with the base and approximately 12 feet (3.7 m) away at double-play depth, the runner should vary or shorten his lead so he can get back to third base safely on a hard-hit ball to the third baseman or pitcher. If the third baseman is playing deep, for example with two outs, the base runner should vary his lead and take several more steps toward home plate *prior* to the pitcher making his movement to the plate.

With a left-handed pitcher, the runner should vary his lead at third base due to the pitcher's back being to the runner. This increased lead can usually be taken regardless of where the third baseman is playing. The runner can be comfortable with more footage because it is rare for a left-handed pitcher to ever turn to throw to third base in today's game.

Secondary Lead at Third Base

A base runner should pay more attention to the quality and distance of his secondary lead at third base than at any other base. When a runner is less than 90 feet (27.4 m) from scoring a run for his team, each step can make a critical difference in being safe or out on many plays.

If the pitcher is in his windup, the runner can take a walking secondary lead that allows him to gain more distance toward home plate. The runner should make the initial crossover step with his left foot, whether in the primary or variable lead, and begin his walk approximately 3 feet (1 m) outside the baseline (see figure 3.12). If the runner is outside the baseline, he can be hit by a batted ball and not be called out. If this happens in the baseline, the runner is called out.

Figure 3.12 The runner takes his secondary lead at third base about 3 feet (1 m) outside the baseline.

The base runner takes 3 to 6 steps toward home plate before the ball is contacted by the hitter, lands in the catcher's mitt, or caroms off the catcher when thrown in the dirt. If the runner must stop, he uses the right foot as the breaking foot, with the toes turned in slightly to the infield (see figure 3.13). This pigeon-toed look with the right foot helps the runner make a stronger stop and turn back toward the base.

Figure 3.13   The runner at third uses his right foot to stop his lead and return to third base.

With a right-handed hitter, the runner at third usually takes a longer lead because the hitter obstructs most of the catcher's view and the pickoff throwing angle. With a left-handed hitter, the runner's secondary lead usually is shorter since the catcher has a clear read of how far the runner has come down the line and an open throwing lane to try to pick off the runner.

When the pitcher is in the stretch, the runner must hold his primary or variable lead a little longer until the pitcher starts the delivery toward home plate. Against a right-handed pitcher, the runner makes sure the pitcher's knee turns and goes to the plate, not toward third base, and then takes a crossover step with the left foot and continues to walk toward the plate for his secondary lead. The secondary lead against a right-handed pitcher should be a minimum of three or four steps. Against a left-handed pitcher, the runner can begin his walk a fraction of a second earlier when the pitcher's front leg is lifted because the pitcher must then throw to home plate. The secondary lead against a left-handed pitcher should be a minimum of four to six steps toward the plate.

Part Two

Running the Bases

Full-speed running with precision is the most difficult aspect for baseball players, and many coaches, to take seriously. Coaches should schedule regular practice sessions to teach running from the batter's box, running through first base, and rounding the bases at full speed with precision. However, it is rare to find these drills regularly conducted in baseball practice.

The lack of fundamental drill work in learning to run full speed when baserunning, especially when leaving the batter's box, is one of the main reasons baseball has become a game of joggers. Too many runners heading to first base and going around the bases jog while the ball is still in play. This area of the game needs to change. A baseball player should always run full speed once he leaves the batter's box until the play is completed.

Base runners must learn and fully understand multiple responsibilities for the benefit of the team. Some of these responsibilities include prereading where defensive players set up, watching where catchers position themselves behind the plate on called pitches, knowing each outfielder's arm strength, paying attention to how coaches motion with their arms as players round the bases, clearly realizing game situations such as the number of outs and the proper reaction when balls are hit into particular areas of the field, and understanding in what situations a runner should tag up or go all the way to the next base before a play is made by the defense. A player who knows these situations well and knows how to react will make the game so much more fun and meaningful for himself and will certainly help his team.

Breaking From the Box

There is no settled theory on how hitters should break from the batter's box. This area of the game is rarely practiced, so there are lots of unknowns regarding the best technique and how to improve quickness when leaving the batter's box. Most hitters are just trying to accelerate as fast as possible after contact.

Right-handed hitters usually move from the batter's box in somewhat of a straight line toward first base. Left-handed hitters move from the batter's box more awkwardly than their right-handed counterparts since their back is to first base and they need to cross over with the left leg to get started. And switch hitters must learn to exit the box using both styles.

When hitters bunt, the way they leave the box depends on how a coach has taught them to set their feet. When a hitter is asked to hit and run or run and hit, once again the feet may set differently than if the hitter was taking a normal swing. And sometimes a hitter will fake bunt and slap the bat at the ball. In this situation, the feet might be still but also could be making a stride when the swing is made.

RIGHT-HANDED HITTER LEAVING THE BATTER'S BOX

A majority of hitters take a stride as the pitch is delivered. However, the angle of the stride differs. Some hitters stride into the pitch, others stride straight to the pitcher, and a few stride a fraction toward third base. This variety means each hitter needs individual attention on the mechanics of leaving the batter's box after making contact to improve the initial steps toward first base.

If a right-handed hitter is trying to fight off an inside fastball, the hitter's balance point may be more toward his lower back or even on his heels. Yet if that same hitter is trying to make contact with a slow breaking ball on the first-base side of the plate, his balance may be toward the front of his feet with the upper body tipping over the plate. The question then is whether the hitter tries to leave the batter's box the same way each time or if it depends on where the pitch is. It is best if the hitter has a similar balance point and departure from the box on all pitches for more consistent running times to first base.

Most right-handed hitters, regardless of the pitch, after taking the swing begin their movement toward first base by retracting the stride foot from 12 to 24 inches (30-60 cm) toward the back of the batter's box. This is the exact opposite of how a hitter should leave the box. By retracting the left foot, the hitter actually starts farther away from first base than when he made contact with the baseball. Unless a right-handed hitter has looked at video extensively or a coach has noticed the retraction of the stride foot, the player probably does not know he actually retracts the stride foot as he begins his run to first base.

Preferably, the hitter should finish with good balance on both feet, slightly over the plate and with the stride foot holding its ground. The back foot then takes the first step directly across the plate and up the first-base line (see figure 4.1). This way the hitter is actually gaining ground on the initial step instead of losing ground.

Figure 4.1 Right-handed hitter leaving the batter's box: *(a)* batter's balanced stance after contact; *(b)* back foot begins to move toward first-base line; *(c)* back foot steps across the plate and up the first-base line; *(d)* front foot strides down first-base line.

Leaving the Right-Handed Batter's Box

OBJECTIVES

The right-handed hitter learns to maintain his balance in the batter's box, which then allows him to step more directly toward first base when leaving the box.

EQUIPMENT

This drill can be practiced anywhere, with or without the hitter swinging a bat. No additional equipment is needed to execute this drill. If there is room to swing, a bat can be used to help simulate leaving the batter's box more realistically. An imaginary batter's box or any markings on a floor can be used.

EXECUTION

Practice swinging the bat with good balance and try to maintain your footing when the stride foot comes down. Start the stride toward first base with as little movement as possible from the stride foot so the back foot can begin to step sooner.

COACHING POINTS

The athlete should remain balanced during the swing. The initial movement after the swing should be with the back foot stepping across the plate instead of the front foot retracting and taking the hitter farther away from first base.

LEFT-HANDED HITTER
LEAVING THE BATTER'S BOX

As with right-handed hitters, most left-handed hitters stride as the pitch is delivered, although the angle may vary. The hitter may stride into the pitch, straight at the pitcher, or even slightly toward first base. Because each hitter is different, the coach must work with each individually to perfect his mechanics when leaving the batter's box after contact and get the most out of his initial steps toward first.

If a left-handed hitter is trying to fight off an inside fastball, the hitter's balance point may be more toward his lower back or even on his heels. In this instance, the hitter may actually fall back toward the first-base dugout a fraction before the left leg crosses over to run to first base. Yet if that same hitter is trying to make contact with a slow breaking ball on the third-base side of the plate, especially from a left-handed pitcher, his balance may be toward the front of his feet with the upper body tipping over the plate. Here, the batter is over home plate and must either take a short step with the right foot to open the body so the back leg can cross over and align the runner to first base, or if the right leg holds its ground, the back leg makes a dramatic crossover step to set up the hitter to run directly to first base.

Some left-handed hitters, as with their right-handed counterparts, regardless of the pitch, after taking the swing begin their run toward first base by retracting the stride foot 6 to 12 inches (15-30 cm) toward the back of the batter's box. This causes slower times to first base. However, many more left-handed hitters than right-handed hitters hold their ground with their stride foot in the box after making contact with the pitch. This may be due to the fact that the left-handed hitter knows he must rotate his body to place it in a more direct line to first base.

A habit some left-handed hitters have after making contact is allowing the back foot to step toward or behind the plate slightly due to their momentum. This helps line up the hitter to run in a straighter line toward first base than if he retracted the stride foot. However, it does place him farther from first base as he begins to run. If a hitter is not going to maintain his balance with both feet after contact, the preferable method is to have the foot fall behind the plate instead of retracting the stride foot.

Spotlight: Ichiro Suzuki

Ichiro Suzuki is the best example of a left-handed hitter who strides in on the pitch, stays over the plate, and then allows the stride foot to open so the back foot can begin the first step sooner and more directly toward first base. Due to his great balance over the plate and ability to exit the box much quicker than almost all other hitters, his running times to first base are impressive. Ichiro usually leads the major leagues in infield hits each season and is still doing so after many years playing at the highest level. History proves athletes' speed diminishes late in their careers, but Ichiro's decline is much less notable as a veteran due to his honed technique in leaving the box as a left-handed hitter.

The best approach to an improved exit from the box and a better running time to first base is to finish the swing balanced on both feet and slightly over the plate with the stride foot holding its ground. The stride foot then swings out, possibly moving sideways instead of retracting back, which opens the body so the back foot can then take an inline step toward first base (see figure 4.2).

Figure 4.2   Left-handed hitter leaving the batter's box: *(a)* batter's balanced stance after contact; *(b)* stride foot swings out to open the body; *(c)* back foot comes across; *(d)* back foot steps in line to first base.

Leaving the Left-Handed Batter's Box

OBJECTIVES

The left-handed hitter learns to maintain his balance in the batter's box, which then allows him to step more directly toward first base when leaving the box.

EQUIPMENT

This drill can be practiced anywhere, with or without a hitter swinging a bat. No special equipment is needed to execute this drill. If there is room to swing, a bat can be used to help simulate leaving the batter's box more realistically. An imaginary batter's box can be used or any markings on a floor.

EXECUTION

Practice swinging the bat with good balance, trying to maintain your footing when the stride foot comes down. Then allow the stride foot to swing out and open the body toward first base, which allows for a clean crossover step.

COACHING POINTS

The athlete should remain balanced during the swing. The initial movement after the swing should be with the back foot instead of allowing the front foot to retract and take the hitter farther away from first base. However, with a left-handed hitter, allowing the stride foot to move out is acceptable.

◇◇◇

SWITCH HITTER LEAVING THE BATTER'S BOX

Working with switch hitters is a lot of fun, but it is a tremendous challenge for a switch hitter to learn a similar approach from both sides of the plate. Switch hitters should try to have the same basic stance, balance points, stride direction, stride length, and finish from both sides of the plate. It is simpler to learn to hit one way than opposite ways.

When most switch hitters leave the batter's box from the opposite side of the plate, they usually do so differently. Coaches should try to correct this when players are young, although experienced switch hitters will benefit from this instruction as well. Encourage switch hitters to practice developing similar movements exiting the batter's box from each side so running times to first base are more consistent.

A switch hitter should practice standing in each batter's box, changing back and forth during practice. He should practice without anyone pitching, swinging the bat over and over, and after each swing take the first three steps toward first base. The hitter should take the time to examine his balance point after swinging at an inside, middle-of-the-plate, and outside pitch. When the bat has gone all the way around to the back and the swing is complete, the hitter should look down to see how his feet are situated and what movements take him into the initial steps toward first base. When a switch hitter takes the time to look at the small movements that make a critical difference in the mechanics of leaving the box, he will begin to improve his ability to exit smoothly and quickly like Ichiro Suzuki.

When a switch hitter in the right-handed batter's box sees a flaw in what his feet are doing, such as the stride foot retracting back toward the third-base dugout like some right-handed hitters do, he should work on a way to keep the stride foot stationary after the swing so the back or right leg makes the initial movement. With that adjustment, his times to first base from the right side will improve. In addition, hitting will improve due to greater balance, which always helps a hitter see every kind of pitch better. The hitter then moves to the left-handed box and takes the time to critique his balance after a complete swing with the bat finishing on the back. The hitter should look down to see where his balance point is at that time and how the feet begin the initial movements to exit the box. In this instance, if the back foot does fall toward the back of home plate the hitter should work on keeping the left foot in its tracks and begin the movement toward first base with the stride foot opening up and allowing for a beautiful crossover step from the back foot.

Switch Hitter Leaving the Batter's Box

OBJECTIVES

The switch hitter learns a similar approach to leaving the batter's box from both sides of the plate.

EQUIPMENT

The switch hitter needs a batter's box and a bat. If an actual batter's box is unavailable, he can practice using an imaginary batter's box or any markings on the ground.

EXECUTION

Stand in the right-handed batter's box and swing. After completing the swing, take the first few steps toward first base. Note your balance point during the swing (imagine an inside pitch, an outside pitch, and a pitch over the plate) and immediately after completing the swing.

Switch to the left-handed batter's box, swing, and take the first few steps toward first base. Again note your balance points. Keep alternating sides and work on finding a similar approach to the first few steps toward first base.

COACHING POINTS

The coach watches for balance during the swing, noting any problems with the first few steps, such as the hitter retracting the front foot and moving farther away from first base. The coach should teach the switch hitter to use a similar approach from both sides of the plate.

Infield Grounders

Infielders are positioned to cut off nearly all ground balls and keep them from running into the outfield. However, good baserunning, by both the hitter–runner and any base runners, can disrupt the timing of the fielders, distract the pitcher, and make it more likely a grounder will roll through, creating the opportunity for extra bases.

The hitter and base runners need to know the game situation, the arm strength and accuracy of the infielders and outfielders, and what to do with this information. A player has just a split second to decide whether or not to advance.

RUNNING TO FIRST BASE ON AN INFIELD GROUND BALL

When a hitter exits the box toward first base on an infield ground ball, the run should be broken into three segments: the initial acceleration of the first 30 feet (9.1 m) toward first base after leaving the batter's box, the 30 feet in which the hitter becomes a sprinter, and the 30 feet to first base in which the runner must concentrate on the first baseman catching the ball. The runner must know how to approach touching first base.

From the Batter's Box Through the First 30 Feet

Hitters vary greatly in the way they leave the batter's box, as covered in chapter 4. But once the hitter turns into a runner trying to reach safely on an infield ground ball, he should immediately transition to a sprinter.

On an infield ground ball, the hitter knows when he leaves the box he is going to run directly through first base unless the throw pulls the first baseman off the bag and into the baseline. The player running down the first-base line should simulate an Olympic sprinter out of the blocks and accelerating toward the finish line tape. The baseball sprinter's tape is first base, and he should try to reach that finish line as quickly as possible.

This is where the development of speed and quickness comes into play. Chapter 12 on speed development offers detailed instruction on how to work toward the physical and mental tools of a sprinter. These tools allow players to improve their sprinting ability when leaving the box and move more efficiently in a direct line to first base and when stealing or running around the bases.

I have experimented with sprinting drills as a player and then as a coach for many years to try to find the best way to turn a hitter into a sprinter once the bat is discarded. I have observed from great sprint coaches such as Tim Bishop, the former Baltimore Orioles coach who trained my son Brian Roberts and helped him become a Major League Baseball all-star as an Orioles infielder and AL base-stealing champion in 2007, and Mark Verstegen, founder and owner of the world renowned Athletes' Performance Institute (where I have worked the past six years) in Phoenix, Arizona, who trained Carl Crawford, a four-time AL base-stealing champion, how to train players to work on their sprint routines.

The hitter should sprint with his head up and, after a quick glance to see if the ball leaves the infield, readjust his eyes to first base. By the time the runner has aligned himself toward the base in the initial three to four steps (see figure 5.1), he should be sprinting, ideally with good form learned from practicing speed and quickness drills like those in chapter 12. Now let's learn what the sprinter does from 30 to 60 feet (9.1-18.3 m) down the line to the base.

Figure 5.1 Batter running from the batter's box after contact.

30 to 60 Feet Down the First-Base Line

The second segment of running to first base on an infield ground ball covers the 30 to 60 feet (9.1-18.3 m) down the first-base line (see figure 5.2). In this area of the basepath, many players can separate themselves from the average runner if they work to increase their speed. During this segment, the player sprints for about 30 to 40 feet (9.1-12.2 m), mimicking the form exhibited by many Olympic sprinters.

To improve speed, players must mentally take the baseball uniform off and put the track uniform on and spend a great deal of time working on sprint mechanics. Olympic sprinters' knees are raised high, whereas many baseball players run from side to side with a lower knee drive. Olympic sprinters push out of the ground straight ahead. The head is level and as steady as that of a deer running across farmland, and the arms drive straight back and forth with the hands coming up to about head high during the run. When the body flows smoothly and with great force in a straight line, an athlete's speed increases. The player should focus on beautiful form and increasing speed. If successful, the runner will be safe at first base more often.

Too often today, if a player feels he can't beat the throw or will definitely be out, he decides to shut down the motor and jog through first base. This is regrettable. Coaches covering base-running drills should encourage athletes to rethink this decision. One problem with this decision is if the athlete decides he is not going to beat the throw and

Figure 5.2   Base runner halfway down the first-base line.

begins to back off the desire to sprint full speed through the base, his recorded time will be much slower across the finish line. This is not a good projection of the athlete in a professional scout's eyes. More importantly, the player will never know if he could have beaten the throw because he slowed down and did not sprint through the base.

The thought of jogging should never enter a player's mind-set. The player has a responsibility to his team and himself to sprint at all times. Maybe by applying pressure he will cause the other team to make a mistake, one not possible if the player was jogging.

Players need to practice their stride length, stride frequency, and form to improve their overall speed. If these are practiced repeatedly, the athlete's speed will increase and he'll place more pressure on the defensive team. Even though it takes a lot of work, increasing his speed should be every athlete's goal.

60 to 90 Feet in the Sprint to First Base

The runner is in full-speed mode by the third segment, having now reached approximately 60 feet (18.3 m) down the first-base line and rapidly approaching the potential end of the race at first base. The athlete is sprinting with his head up and eyes locked on the first baseman and the general area of first base (see figure 5.3).

At this point the runner begins to visualize, not guess, whether the first baseman is going to have to move off the base to attempt to catch an off-target throw. The runner is reading the first baseman's

Figure 5.3 Base runner sprints with his head up and his eyes on the first baseman.

feet as the sprint to the base continues. If the first baseman's feet begin to move, the runner has to decide where to go. The runner can continue through the base with the sprint or try to make a last-second judgment to slide to one side of the bag or the other.

If the runner reads that the first baseman is going to stay on the base, then he should continue to sprint through the base. The stride length should remain the same unless the final step needs to be cut down to touch the nearest portion, or home plate side, of the base.

A runner should always look at the base as his foot is touching the bag (see figure 5.4). When the runner looks down at the base as the foot is touching the bag the head should begin to turn right to see if the ball has been overthrown or ricocheted toward the fence line or dugout. If the runner sees the baseball to the right and feels

Figure 5.4 Base runner touching first base: *(a)* Base runner looks down at the base as he makes contact and then *(b)* looks right to see if he can advance farther.

there is an opportunity to advance, he can slow down and make the turn sooner. The runner should never rely on the first-base coach to make the decision whether to make the turn and possibly go to second base. However, the first-base coach should help the runner with a verbal cue, for example, "stay here, stay here," which tells the runner to not make the turn. In this case, if the runner does take one or two steps toward second base, he should return to the base as soon as possible.

If a runner does not make any attempt to move toward the next base on an overthrow, then he can return to the base at his own pace with no concern of being tagged out. However, if the runner begins the commitment toward second base, he must continue that commitment or return to first base without being tagged with the baseball to remain safe.

Sprint to First Base

OBJECTIVES

The hitter sprints in the initial steps out of the box and through the bag each time the ball is hit to an infielder.

EQUIPMENT

A base, a placeholder (if the drill is done inside), or a square drawn in the dirt for the hitter to touch and enough space to sprint the length of the first-base path. This drill can be done using a bat and taking a full swing or without a bat by taking an imaginary swing.

EXECUTION

Practice swinging the bat or use an imaginary swing with good balance and try to maintain your footing when the stride foot comes down. Start the stride toward first base with as little movement as possible from the stride foot so the back foot can begin to step sooner. Practice sprinting through the base each time, making sure to hit the home plate side of the base, and immediately look right to see if the ball got past the first baseman.

COACHING POINTS

The athlete should look to see where the ball has gone immediately after the ball leaves the bat. From then on, the attention is toward first base, and the goal is to sprint the entire distance until reaching the bag. The player should look to the right once he has touched the base.

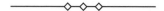

RUNNING BETWEEN THE BASES ON AN INFIELD GROUND BALL

A runner on first, second, or third base has many decisions to make before the delivery of the pitch and after the batter makes contact. The base runner is taking a lead. When the baseball is hit on the ground in the infield, the base runner must anticipate movement before he actually places the body in motion.

Anticipation is key before the pitch is made. Base runners should always anticipate what they will do if the ball is hit on the ground in the infield and have different reads depending on where in the infield the ball goes.

The base runner must know the positioning of the infielders. The runner views the positioning of both the right and left infielders and knows their depth. Knowing their positioning helps determine where the infielder might throw the ball if fielded. As a runner processes this information with anticipation, he has good knowledge of the infield setup prior to the pitch. If contact is made, the runner already knows how he will approach the next bag no matter where the ball is thrown. If the ball is not put in play, the runner can safely return to the base.

Base runners should view the ball out of the pitcher's hand, track the ball during flight, and read the ball off the bat. Runners need to read *white* (or baseball) out of the pitcher's hand and off the bat. If the ball quickly hits *green* (grass) off the bat, the runner reacts according to where the infielder makes the play. As the runner moves to the next base, he has anticipated where the infielder will make the throw, reads the throw, and reacts to the play. If white (baseball) is read going upward slightly off the bat, the runner must react a fraction slower since the ball could be caught in the air.

Runner on First Base, No Outs or One Out

With an infield grounder, no outs or one out, and the runner on first base, the runner should read the ball (white) off the bat and decide if he will go into second base sliding or standing up. If the defensive player decides to deliver the ball to second base, the runner should hit the dirt and try to cleanly break up the double-play possibility. A runner can always use a pop-up slide to help with his possible movement toward third base if the ball is mishandled by the infielder or thrown away either in front of or behind the runner. On the final few steps before reaching second base, the runner must always prepare to make a turn if the ball happens to scoot past the infielder into the outfield. He should look down and touch the base and then look up and pick up the third-base coach in case the grounder that started in the infield quickly found its way to the outfield grass.

Runner on First Base, Two Outs

With an infield grounder, two outs, and the runner on first base, the runner should read the ball (white) off the bat and have a much better jump than with no outs or one out. The runner does not have to be concerned with the ball in the air so he is definitely moving toward second base on contact. If the runner has anticipated contact well off the bat and the ball is thrown to second base to try to force this runner, the play should be much closer because the runner has a very good jump.

The runner should prepare to slide into second base until he reads that the ball has been thrown behind him to first base to try for the third out. Again, the runner must prepare for the infielder to mishandle the ball or make a poor throw in front of the runner at second base or behind the runner to first base.

Runner on Second Base, No Outs or One Out

With an infield grounder, no outs or one out, and a runner on second base, the runner should anticipate reading the ball (white) off the bat to three areas of the infield before committing to movement toward third base. The baseball could be hit behind the runner on the right side of the infield, directly up the middle, or in front of the runner on the left side of the infield (see figure 5.5).

Seeing the ball off the bat well is important after the runner has visualized where the ball might be hit. The runner is not guessing but is coached to look (visualize) for the ball to be hit on the left side of the infield (to the runner's right side).

In his reaction process, the runner knows if the ball is hit to his right, he will not proceed to third base unless he advances after the ball is thrown across the infield or the ball at the last second scoots off a glove or is mishandled by the defender. By looking for the ball to come off the bat to the runner's right side, the runner normally will visually read the baseball more clearly and stay at second base.

The concept of looking for the baseball on the right side of the runner and the left side of the infield is a change from what I first learned. As a young baseball player I was taught to look for the ball on the right side of the infield. However, as I began coaching, I found it was easier for the runner to advance from second if he looked for the hit to the left side of the infield. I taught my runners to look to their right side and the left side of the infield to read the baseball. This cut down on baserunning mistakes on a ball hit in the infield.

If the ball is hit behind the runner and far enough away from the pitcher to be fielded by the first or second baseman, the runner can delay his reaction slightly and still advance to third base. Therefore,

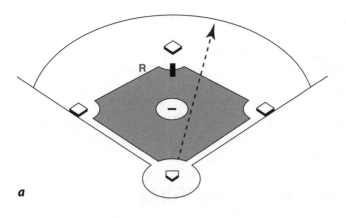

a

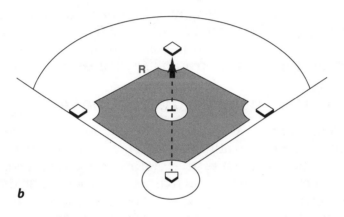

b

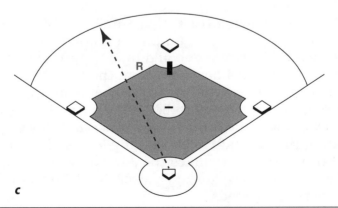

c

Figure 5.5 Three areas of the infield where a ground ball might be hit with a runner on second base and no outs or one out: *(a)* right side of infield behind the runner; *(b)* directly up; *(c)* left side of infield in front of the runner.

there is little need for a runner to focus on the ball being hit to the right side of the infield.

The ball hit up the middle is the toughest read due to the defensive possibilities. If the pitcher fields the ball at the last second, the runner must still be under control and close enough to second base to return safely if the pitcher makes a throw. However, the runner must also be prepared for a ball hit up the middle not fielded by the pitcher but still behind or to the runner's left side to be able to advance to third base safely.

Runner on Second Base, Two Outs

With an infield grounder and two outs, the runner on second base has more freedom to take a little more daring leads than with no outs or one out. On most infield ground balls hit with two outs, the infielder will try to make the play at first base and not worry about the runner trying to advance to third base. The base runner should read the baseball off the bat and sprint to third base, prepared for the opportunity to make a turn and score if the play is muffed.

Runner on Third Base, No Outs or One Out

On an infield grounder with no outs or one out, the runner at third base should anticipate reading the ball (white) off the bat in a downward action where white hits green (grass) almost immediately. The runner is either reading the ball to know whether to advance toward home plate or is moving on contact. These situations change when the infield is back, partially up and back, or playing up to try to cut off the runner at the plate.

Infielders Back

With all infielders playing back, the runner at third base has an excellent chance of scoring on an infield ground ball without even going on contact. The runner should take a standing lead equal to the distance of the third baseman from the base and take a controlled walk toward home plate as the pitcher delivers. If the pitcher is left-handed, the runner can walk farther down the line due to the pitcher's back being to the runner. The runner must know his comfort distance from the base after the walking lead so he can return to the base safely if the hitter takes the pitch or swings through it so the catcher does not have an easy pickoff throw to third base. Let's look at some possible reads.

The initial read is the ball hit directly at the third baseman. In this situation, the infielder is still close enough to home plate to either make the throw to the plate or first base. The runner needs to read the ball immediately off the bat to ensure a good jump and force the third baseman to go to first base to get an out. However, if the runner does not have a good jump, he should stay at third base, especially with no one out.

The second read off the bat is the ball hit directly up the middle of the diamond. The runner should be under control with the secondary lead to make sure if the pitcher does field the ball the only play the pitcher has is to first base. If the ball continues past the pitcher, the runner should score easily.

The baseball hit on the ground in the infield grass toward first base, the second baseman, or the shortstop should be the easiest read for a runner at third base with none or one out. The runner is patient to read the ball is clear of the pitcher and advances easily to score.

First and Third Basemen Up, Middle Infielders Back or Halfway Back

If half the infield is playing up, the runner at third must read the ball (white) off the bat much more precisely to prevent running into an out at home plate or being caught in a rundown between third and home. The runner must hesitate a split second longer to see if the ball is hit in the area where the first baseman, third baseman, or pitcher can make the play. Each of these fielders is playing on the edge of the grass, which gives them a very short throw to the plate. The runner should read if the first or third baseman has to dive to make the play. When the fielder is heading to the ground, the runner should be advancing toward the plate unless the ball is hit exceptionally hard.

If the runner reads the ball well off the bat and the ball will definitely be fielded by the shortstop or second baseman, the runner is able to advance easily toward home plate. However, this is sometimes a difficult read with the corner infielders playing in, so the runner must hesitate for a split second before committing toward home plate.

Infielders Up

With a runner on third base and the infielders all playing up on the edge of the infield grass, for the runner to advance toward home plate he must read the ball going through the infield. He might be able to score if the ball takes an unusually high bounce immediately in front of home plate. If the third-base coach informs the runner to go on contact, this means on any ground ball the player is trying to advance toward home plate.

A runner should know he is not advancing on a ball fielded by the pitcher or any infielder. The throw will be so short there is little chance of being safe. The runner should have an abnormally short primary lead, whether against a right- or left-handed pitcher, and take a controlled and short secondary lead. If the ball is hit on the ground, the runner holds his ground. If the ball is hit to the left side of the infield and is fielded at third or short or by the pitcher, the runner retreats back to third base. If the ball is hit on the right side of the infield, the runner continues to have an adequate lead off third base as the ball is fielded by either the first or second baseman.

A ball may be misplayed or go under or by an infielder when he is playing on the edge of the infield grass. A runner should be looking for the ball to bounce away or go through or under the glove and the opportunity to advance.

If a coach has asked the runner to move on contact on a ball hit on the ground, the runner can anticipate and cheat a small amount to get an excellent jump. In this instance, the runner is hoping the ball is hit to the side of an infielder, not directly at an infielder, so the throw to the plate is more difficult.

Runners on First and Second Base, No Outs or One Out

On an infield ground ball with no outs or one out, the runners on first and second base must try to advance. Each runner should anticipate sliding into the next base until he has read the ball (white) off the bat and determined where the ball may be played. Then he decides whether to stand up or slide. Once again, the runner must see if the ball is fielded cleanly or muffed before he knows definitely what his approach will be when arriving at the next base.

Runners on First, Second, and Third Base, No Outs or One Out

With no outs or one out on an infield ground ball, the runners on first, second, and third base must try to advance. Each runner anticipates sliding into the next base until he has read the ball (white) off the bat and knows where the ball may be played. Then he decides whether to stand up or slide. The runner must see if the ball is fielded cleanly or muffed before knowing definitely what his approach will be when arriving at the next base.

Runners on First and Third Base, No Outs or One Out

On an infield grounder with no outs or one out, the runner on first must advance, but the runner at third must read the play before advancing. Usually in this situation the infield will play with the third baseman on the edge of the grass and the first baseman holding the runner. The first baseman moves to the edge of the grass after the pitch, and the middle infielders play back for a possible double-play ball. The exception is when the winning run is at third base and all infielders are playing on the edge of the grass to make the play at the plate.

On a ground ball, the runner at first base must try to advance. The runner at first should always anticipate sliding into the base but will read the play and make that decision based on where the ball is thrown. The runner at third base does not have to advance so he will read the ground ball and make the decision based on where the ball is hit, how hard the ball is hit, and where the defensive player decides to make the play.

Runners on Second and Third Base, No Outs or One Out

With no outs or one out, the runners on second and third base do not have to advance on an infield ground ball. The score of the game, number of outs, and the kind of hitter at the plate determine where each infielder is playing and where he would like to make the next play.

The lead runner at third base anticipates what decision to make after seeing the ball (white) come off the bat at a downward angle onto the grass. Unless the runner is going on contact, trying to advance on any ground ball, the runner must know where each infielder is playing, read the speed and angle of the ball off the bat, and then decide whether to attempt to move toward home plate or stay at third base. The runner does have the luxury of not having to attempt to go anywhere if there is not a good chance of safely crossing the plate.

The runner at second base must read the player at third base, never taking his eyes off the lead runner, so he can make a good decision on whether to stay or move up if the opportunity arises. However, the runner at second base also has the luxury of not having to move up on any ground ball hit to the infield.

Runners on Any Base, Two Outs

With two outs, the runners on base, in almost any game situation, should have made one of two decisions. Unless the bases are loaded, they are staying at the base if the ball is hit in an area of the infield where it is best to be patient. The runner sits still and sees if the infielder can make the play and throw to first base to get the hitter out. If the infielder cannot make the attempted out at first base, then each runner is safe and the inning continues with two outs.

The second decision is to take an excellent jump and move toward the next base when the ball is contacted. The runners do not have to be concerned with a line drive grabbed on a great play or a caught fly ball because there are two outs in the inning. However, as the play unfolds, each runner must decide if he can continue to round the bases aggressively or must watch closely to see if the third out is not made. Then he would need to pull up at a base safely so the inning can continue.

Ground Ball Down the Line to the Outfield (Potential Extra-Base Hit)

On a ground ball just inside the foul line, the hitter is not sure when he leaves the box if there will be a play at a base or the bouncing baseball is a potential single or double. If at the last second the ball does move past the corner infielder and into the outfield, the base runner must make a split-second decision on whether to continue to sprint as he rounds first base or return to first base.

The hitter begins to run down the first-base line like a sprinter, thinking he will run straight through first base to try to beat an infield single. As the hitter hustles to first base, he is able to see approximately 30 feet (~9 m) down the line that the ball went under the glove of the infielder and rolled into the outfield.

Now the runner must veer out of the first-base line approximately 10 to 12 feet (3-3.7 m) to make a quick turn as directly as possible toward second base after touching first base (see figure 5.6). With either foot, the runner hits the corner of first base on the second-base side of the bag and the side nearest home plate. He pushes off this corner of the bag using the left side of the body to pull slightly downward through the curve to stay almost in a straight line toward second base. The runner now decides if he will continue on to second base or make an abrupt stop and return to first base.

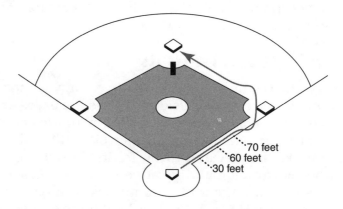

Figure 5.6   Runner making the turn at first base on an extra-base ground ball.

The runner must look at first base to make sure he touches the base. As soon as he sees his foot touch the base, he looks up to find the baseball and the defensive player and quickly calculates what his chances are of arriving safely at the next base. Previously during infield practice, the runner should have been watching the arm strength, accuracy, and quickness of the outfielders so he can recall that information in a millisecond and decide whether to continue to run. This is one of the fun aspects about running the bases after a base hit. The runner can challenge the defensive team and see who comes up the winner when it comes to taking an extra base or two.

Runners at Different Bases

OBJECTIVES

Learn to anticipate the ball (white) coming off the bat and hitting the grass immediately. Practice making decisions from different bases with no other runners, with runners in front, and with runners behind when the ball is hit in the infield.

EQUIPMENT

Bases at first, second, and third and baseballs.

EXECUTION

All infielders, a catcher, and a pitcher play defense. The pitcher throws live batting practice to a teammate or coach. The ball is hit to infielders playing up, halfway, or back as base runners read and react to the ball off the bat and to the plays the infielders make. The coach sets up different defensive and offensive scenarios for every practice.

COACHING POINTS

Athletes learn to anticipate the ball (white) coming off the bat at a downward angle in multiple directions. Runners learn to read, not guess, the ball with different outs, the positioning of the infielders, and the reactions of the runners in front of them.

Outfield Flies

When the hitter exits the box and begins to run toward first base on a fly ball to the outfield, he should immediately turn into a sprinter and always run the play as if he had hit an extra-base hit. Many times games change quickly by a hitter sprinting to and around first base as a fly ball is chased by an outfielder, only to have the ball unexpectedly fall in safely, allowing the hitter to end up on second or third base.

SPRINTING TO FIRST AND BEGINNING TO ROUND THE BASE

Hitters vary greatly in how they run down the first-base line when they hit a fly ball into the outfield. Too many runners jog as if the ball has already been caught and they are out. A runner should never assume a ball is going to be caught. It is the runner's responsibility to always sprint and allow the play to unfold.

As a runner leaves the plate area on a fly ball and breaks the halfway point toward first base, he should be preparing to make a very short turn to the right to round first base (see figure 6.1). Often runners exaggerate the turn out into the grass, which slows down

Figure 6.1 Base runner beginning to make the turn at first base.

their running time to first base and beyond. If an athlete runs to first base in an average of 4.2 seconds after contact, then he should touch the base as he rounds the bag in approximately 4.5 to 4.6 seconds. If there is more than a 0.4 second differential, then the turn is too large or the athlete is just not sprinting on the turn.

RUNNING BETWEEN BASES ON AN OUTFIELD FLY BALL

A runner on first, second, or third base has many decisions to make before the delivery of the pitch and after the batter makes contact. The base runner is taking a lead. When the baseball is hit in the air to the outfield, the base runner must anticipate his possible movements before he actually places the body in motion.

Anticipation is key before the pitch is made. Base runners should always anticipate what they will do if the ball is hit in the air to the outfield and have different reads depending on where in the outfield the ball goes.

The base runner must know the positioning of the outfielders—straightaway, gap, pull, or offside—and their depth. Outfielders' positioning affects whether they are able to catch a fly ball or make a strong throw on an advancing runner. As a runner processes this information with anticipation, he has a good idea of the outfield setup prior to the pitch. If contact is made and the runner has begun movement toward the next bag, he should know almost immediately if he can advance more than one base because of the outfield alignment. If the ball is not put in play on the pitch, the runner returns to the base and once again views the outfield to check for any alignment changes.

Base runners should view the ball out of the pitcher's hand, track the ball during flight, and read the ball off the bat. Runners need to read white (or baseball) out of the pitcher's hand and off the bat. If the base runner sees white upward off the bat, he can react according to where the outfielders are playing. As the runner moves to the next base, he anticipates during his initial steps where the outfielder will make the throw, reads the throw as well as possibly his third-base coach, and reacts to the defensive play. If white (baseball) is read going upward slightly off the bat, the runner may react a fraction slower than he would like just to make sure the ball is not caught.

Runner on First Base, No Outs or One Out

As a base runner takes his secondary lead at first base, he watches for contact by the hitter. If the ball is hit in the air to the outfield with no outs or one out, the runner must read the ball to its destination in the outfield and be ready to handle one of many scenarios. Let's look at several of the most common in this situation.

Fly Ball of Average Depth From Left Center Field to Left Foul Line

An outfield fly ball is hit where the center or left fielder can make a routine play, and the runner knows almost immediately the outfielder has an opportunity to catch the ball for an out. If the ball is hit to medium depth in left field, on the line in left field, or to left center field, the runner can possibly get two-thirds of the way to second base and be prepared to go either way depending on whether the ball is caught. If the catch is made, the runner quickly retreats to first base. If the ball falls, the runner is very close to second base and can move into second and possibly advance to third.

Fly Ball From Deep Left Center Field to Left Foul Line

An outfield fly ball is hit deep to the outfield anywhere from left center field to the left-field foul line, and the runner feels the outfielder has an excellent chance to catch the ball. The runner must quickly decide whether it is best to go all the way to second base and stay with the foot on the bag until the ball is caught (not allowing both feet to go beyond second base) or return to first base and tag up.

If the runner decides to go to second base, he should place the right foot on the base and the left foot on the third-base side of second base (see figure 6.2). This opens the runner's chest to the right or outfield side, which allows him to see the ball easily in left field. The base runner can quickly advance toward third base if the ball falls safely.

The runner is in an athletic position so he can quickly reverse pivot without completely going to the third-base side of second base with both feet. When reversing pivot, the runner leaves the right foot touching second base so the umpire knows

Figure 6.2 Base runner at second watching for the play on the fly ball to deep left center field. The base runner waits in an athletic position, his right foot on second base and his left foot on the third-base side of second.

the runner has tagged the base as he reverses directions and heads back to first base. The base runner must know that if he takes both feet beyond the next base, in this case second base, he must retag the base on his way back. This is the primary reason I encourage runners to go to the base, keep one foot on the base, and just reverse pivot if the ball is caught in deep left field. This way the umpire should clearly see that the runner handled it correctly if there is an appeal by the defense.

If the runner decides soon after contact that the outfield fly ball is going to be deep but most likely catchable, he may immediately return to first base to tag up. If he does this, the first-base coach should stop the hitter short of the base so the runner and hitter do not cross paths. If a hitter rounding first base passes a base runner coming back to first base and the ball drops fairly inside the play-ing field or goes over the fence for a would-be home run, the hitter is always called out for passing the base runner.

The runner may decide to tag at first base and either try to advance or bluff an advance right after the catch. In this situation, if the runner is not sure he will be able to advance all the way to the next base, he can begin to sprint toward second base with his head up and read the flight of the ball coming from the outfielder's hand. Often because of the distance of the throw, the runner can go halfway to second base before making a final decision. If the flight of the ball is strong and right on the next base, the runner may want to stop and return to the initial base. If the outfielder has poor arm strength or the throw is off, the runner can read the flight of the ball and make a decision very late to continue to the base.

Fly Ball From Shallow Left Center Field to Left Foul Line

A shallow outfield fly ball is hit anywhere from left center to the left-field foul line. The runner must move from his secondary lead to approximately halfway between the bases to see if the ball is caught or drops. The runner should read the flight of the ball and not guess whether the ball will drop.

A quality outfielder who sees he will not make the catch some-times will place his glove up, as if he is going to make the catch, as a defensive decoy. This is why the runner must read the ball and not the actions of the outfielder trying to hold the runner between the bases until he can retrieve the ball.

Fly Ball in Foul Territory Along the Outfield Left-Field Line

When a fly ball down the outfield left-field line is definitely foul, the runner should always return to the base to tag up. Since a runner can advance on a caught foul fly ball only if he tags up, there is no reason for the runner to hang out between the bases. Once the catch is made along the outfield left-field line, the runner can go a good distance off the base to see if he wants to advance to second base due to the long distance of the throw needed.

Fly Ball of Average Depth From Left Center Field to Right Foul Line

An outfield fly of average depth hit anywhere from left center field to the right-field foul line is a difficult scenario for the runner on first base. The runner can't be off the base very far when the play on the ball is made. Most outfielders like to throw. When a runner wanders very far off the base in this situation, outfielders may try to throw behind the runner to first base to see if they can turn a double play. The runner should still be off the base one-third to one-half the distance toward second base but remain aware he may need to return to the base quickly if the outfielder decides to make a throw.

Fly Ball From Deep Left Center Field to Right Foul Line

A fly ball is hit deep to the outfield anywhere from left center field to the right-field foul line, and the runner feels the outfielder has an excellent chance to catch the ball. The runner must quickly decide whether it is best to go all the way to second base and stay with the foot on the base until the ball is caught (not allowing both feet to go beyond second base) or return to first base and tag up.

If the runner decides to go to second base, he should place the right foot on second base and the left foot on the third-base side of second when the ball is in left center field. If the ball is in right center field or right field, the runner should place his right foot on the base and left foot closer to third base. This opens the runner's chest to the outfield so he can see the ball easily. The ball will be closer to first base when caught, so the runner may decide that going all the way to second base is too far since the throw after the catch would be shorter than from the left-field side. However, wherever the base runner decides to go while seeing if the catch is made, he can quickly advance toward third base if the ball falls safely.

The runner is in an athletic position so he can reverse and head back toward first base without completely going to the third-base side of the base with both feet. The runner quickly pivots and heads back to first base whether he set up at or just short of second base.

If the runner decides soon after contact that the outfield fly ball is going to be deep but most likely catchable, he may immediately return to first base to tag up. If he does this, the first-base coach must stop the hitter short of the base so the runner and hitter do not cross paths.

The runner tags at first base and either tries to advance or bluffs an advance right after the catch. If the runner is not sure he is able to advance all the way to the next base, he can begin to sprint toward second base with his head up and read the flight of the ball coming from the outfielder's hand. Because of the distance of the throw, the runner can go halfway to second base before making a final decision. If the ball flight is strong and right on the next base, the runner may want to stop and return to the base. If the outfielder has poor arm strength or the throw is off, the runner can read the flight of the ball and make the decision very late to continue on to the base.

Fly Ball From Shallow Left Center Field to Right Foul Line

A shallow outfield fly ball is hit anywhere from left center to the right-field foul line. The runner must move from his secondary lead to approximately one-third to one-half the distance between the bases to see if the ball is caught or drops. The runner should read the flight of the ball and not guess whether the ball will drop. The closer the ball is hit to the right fielder, the less distance the runner at first base wanders from the base on a short fly ball.

Sometimes the outfielder who sees he will not make the catch will put up his glove as if he will. This is why the runner must read the ball, not the outfielder's actions. The runner does not want to fall for the outfielder's decoy maneuver and hold up between the bases instead of advancing.

Fly Ball in Foul Territory Along the Outfield Right-Field Line

When the runner determines that an outfield fly ball down the right-field line will be foul, he should always return to first base to tag up. Since a runner can advance on a caught foul fly ball only if he tags up, there is no reason for the runner to hang out between the bases. Once the catch is made along the outfield right-field line, the runner can go a short distance off the base to see if he wants to advance to second base due to the long distance of the throw needed. Since the foul ball is along the right-field foul line, it usually has to be very deep for the runner to advance.

Runner on Second Base Only, No Outs or One Out

With a runner on second base with first and third base empty and less than two outs, the runner wants to do all he can to advance to third on a fly ball to the outfield. A runner on third has many more ways to score and help his team than a runner on second base.

As discussed, the runner must know the depth and left-to-right positioning of the outfielders, watch to see at what angle the ball is caught, and know the defensive player's arm strength to make the quick and sometimes risky decision to advance under various fly-ball scenarios.

Fly Ball of Average Depth to Outfield From Foul Line to Foul Line

When a fly ball is hit to the outfield so that any of the outfielders can make a routine play, the runner knows almost immediately the outfielder has an opportunity to catch the ball for an out. If the ball is hit to medium depth, the runner can possibly go one-third of the way toward third base and read the play. If this ball is caught, the runner returns to second base quickly. If the ball falls, the runner can move at least to third base.

Deep Fly Ball to Outfield

When a fly ball is hit deep anywhere to the outfield, the runner may feel the outfielder has a chance to catch the ball. If there is still some doubt the outfielder will make the play, the base runner needs to quickly decide if it is best to go all the way or almost all the way to third base and stay with the foot on the bag until the ball is caught (not allowing both feet to go beyond third base) or return to second base and tag up.

If the runner has some doubt about whether the ball will be caught deep in the outfield, he may decide to go to third base and hang out until he sees the ball caught. The base runner places his right foot on third base and his left foot on the home plate side off third base if the ball is very deep to the left-field corner. This opens his chest to the ball. If the ball is hit to deep left center field, center field, right center field, or the deepest part of the right-field corner, the left foot is on the base and the right foot is on the ground so the chest and eyes are open to the play.

It takes an aggressive and knowledgeable base runner to go to the next base and wait for the catch. Many runners feel going to third base is too far if the ball is caught in center field, right field, or left center field since the throw after the catch is shorter than if the ball were hit deep to a corner. Wherever the base runner decides to go between the bases to see if the catch is made, he can quickly advance toward third base if the ball falls safely.

The runner maintains an athletic position so he can reverse and head back toward second base without completely going on the other side of third base with both feet. The runner can quickly reverse pivot and head back to second base whether he sets up at or just short of third base.

If soon after contact the base runner decides the outfield fly ball is going to be deep but most likely catchable, he may immediately return to second base to tag up. When the runner tags up, he should have his chest open to the side of the field where the baseball is caught. Immediately after the catch the runner should look up for help from the third-base coach on whether to continue to third or stop if the outfielder is making a great throw behind him. If the ball is in left center field or toward the left-field line, the runner can read the throw himself and make the final decision. If the throw is strong and right on target to third base, the runner may want to stop and return to second base. If the outfielder has poor arm strength or the throw is off, the runner can read the flight of the ball and decide very late to continue to the base.

Shallow Fly Ball to Outfield

A shallow fly ball is hit anywhere in the outfield. The base runner at second must move from his secondary lead to approximately one-third to one-half the distance between the bases to see if the ball is caught or drops. The runner should read the flight of the ball and not guess whether the ball will drop. The closer to the infield dirt the shallow fly ball is hit, the less distance the runner at second base should wander since the fielder's throw is very short.

The runner should not be tricked by a decoy maneuver by the out-fielder. An experienced outfielder who knows he won't be able to make the catch may raise his glove as if he will be able to catch the ball. The runner doesn't read the outfielder's actions, he reads the ball.

Fly Ball in Foul Territory Along the Outfield Right- or Left-Field Line

When the base runner determines an outfield fly ball down the right- or left-field line will be foul, he should always return to second base to tag up. Since a runner can advance on a caught foul fly ball only if he tags up, there is no reason for the runner to hang out between the bases. Once the catch is made in foul territory in the outfield, the runner goes a short distance off second base, looks to the third-base coach for help, and decides if he wants to try to advance to third base due to the long distance of the throw needing to be made.

If along the left-field foul line, the foul ball usually has to be very deep for the runner to advance. The base runner may be able to advance if the left fielder has to run toward the stands or fence since this means the outfielder must stop and turn to throw back to third base, which opens up the possibility for the base runner to advance. If the ball is along the right-field foul line, it must be thrown a much farther distance to third base so the runner wants to read the catch well and force the outfielder to make a strong throw to third base.

Runner on Third Base, No Outs or One Out

When a fly ball is hit anywhere in the outfield, fair or foul, the runner at third base should always return to the base to tag up regardless of the depth of the fly ball. This prepares the runner for any situation in the outfield, whether the ball is caught or falls to the ground safely.

If the ball is hit in fair territory anywhere from the left-field line to the right-field fence, the runner should set up with his left foot on the base and his right foot out front on the ground (see figure 6.3), which opens the chest and head to the field and helps the runner better read the ball. Also, this gives the runner a balanced sprinter's stance to come off the base toward home plate when the ball is caught or lands safely.

If the ball is hit in foul territory down the left-field line, the runner sets up with his right foot on the base and left foot on the ground in front of the base toward home plate (see figure 6.4). The chest and head are open toward the stands or fence, which gives the runner a better view of the ball being caught or landing in foul territory.

After the ball is caught or lands safely, the runner takes one step toward home plate and looks to get help from the third-base coach, who should be down the line reading the flight of the ball. The runner can read the flight of the ball being thrown by the right or center fielder for a split second but should turn over the responsibility of deciding to score or return to the base to the third-base coach. A runner sprints faster if he has all parts of his body directed toward his end target.

Figure 6.3 Base runner at third in sprinter's stance with his left foot on third base and his right foot in front, ball hit in fair territory to the outfield.

Figure 6.4 Base runner at third with his right foot on third base and his left foot on the ground toward home plate, ball hit foul down the left-field line.

Multiple Runners on Base

We covered what a runner should do at each base in most fly-ball situations. However, when multiple runners are on base working together to advance, a lot more decisions come into play.

When multiple runners are on base, most of the time the primary decision on how runners will react is on the shoulders of the lead runner. For example, with runners on first and second base and a fly ball to the outfield, the lead runner is at second base. The only way the trailing runner can advance is to read the lead runner and try to head to the next base if he tries to advance. However, in some situations the runner on first base will go almost all the way to second base to wait to see if the catch is made in the outfield, but the runner on second base is only a short distance in front of the trailing runner so he can tag up if the ball is caught. In this case, one runner may have made a mistake. But with multiple runners on base many scenarios are possible.

The one time the trailing runner may be the primary decision maker is when runners are on first and third, a short fly ball—fair or foul—is hit to the outfield, and the runner on first base wants to force a throw to second by trying to advance. This may give the runner on third a chance to score if the trailing runner can draw the throw to second base.

The outfielder is probably catching the ball in an area where he knows the runner on third base will not try to advance so he doesn't make an immediate throw to the cutoff man between the outfielder and home plate. The runner at first base anticipates that the outfielder is thinking the runner on third will not try to advance, even though the runner may fake advancing, and the outfielder may hold the ball for an instant longer than usual. The outfielder then sees the runner on first trying to advance to second and makes a long throw toward second base, which may give the runner at third a chance to score.

Runners on Any Base With Two Outs

With two outs, the runners on base, in almost any game situation, should have made the decision prior to contact by the hitter to sprint as if the outfielder was not even there and the catch will not be made. In the case of a ball hit directly at an outfielder, many players jog instead of sprint, as if saying there's no need to run hard since it's the third out. The runner should always sprint to home plate from third base or around the bases from second or first, keeping his head up to see the play in front of him or watching the third-base coach if the play is behind him. Base runners want to advance as far as possible, realizing they still may have to stop at a base prior to scoring. This depends on where the ball is hit in the outfield and how well the outfielder returns the ball to the infield. The runners focus on sprinting until the ball is caught or thrown to the infield. Then they or the third-base coach make the decision to pull up at a base safely so the inning can continue.

Fly Ball Down the Line, Potential Extra-Base Hit

On a fly ball just inside the foul line, the hitter is not sure when he leaves the box if there will be a play at a base or the ball is a potential single or double. If at the last second the ball does move past the corner infielder and into the outfield, the base runner must make a split-second decision whether to continue to sprint as he rounds first base or return to first.

The hitter begins to run down the first-base line like a sprinter, with the idea of running straight through first base to try to beat out an infield single. As the hitter hustles to first base, he is able to see approximately 30 feet (~9 m) down the line that the ball went over the glove of the third baseman or first baseman and rolled into the outfield.

Now the runner must veer out of the first-base line approximately 10 to 12 feet (3-3.7 m) to make a quick turn as directly as possible toward second base after touching first. With either foot, the runner hits the corner of first base on the second-base side of the bag and the side nearest home plate. He pushes off this corner of the bag using the left side of his body to pull slightly downward through the curve to stay almost in a straight line toward second base. The runner must now decide if he will continue on to second base or make an abrupt stop and return to first base.

The runner must look at first base to make sure he touches the base. As soon as he sees his foot touch the base, he looks up to find the baseball and the defensive player and quickly calculates his chances of arriving safely at the next base. During warm-ups, the runner should have been watching for the outfielders' arm strength, accuracy, and quickness so that information can be recalled in a millisecond and he can decide whether to continue. This is a fun aspect of baserunning after a base hit. The runner can challenge the defensive team and see who comes up the winner when it comes to taking an extra base or two.

Reacting to an Outfield Fly Ball

OBJECTIVES

Learn when to go all the way to the next base to see if the fly ball is caught or lands safely, when it's best to go halfway between the bases, and when to go back to the base and tag up, expecting to advance to the next base after the outfielder makes the catch.

EQUIPMENT

Bases, fungo, baseballs.

EXECUTION

Runners take positions on the bases and prepare to work on all game situations. The coach hits fly balls to the outfield, both in fair and foul territory. For each fly ball, runners are told the number of outs. Runners decide where to set up on the base and work on how to react after the ball is caught or drops safely.

COACHING POINTS

Runners learn to read the ball off the bat well and make mature decisions about how far to go toward the next base while waiting to see if the play is made or whether to return to the base immediately, knowing it is highly likely the ball will be caught and they may be able to tag and move to the next base. With multiple runners, except with runners on first and third, the focus is on the lead runner to read his reactions. With runners on first and third, each runner may move independently.

Part Three

Base Stealing

Base stealing is such an exciting part of the game of baseball. It's an area of expertise separate from base running. An athlete who wants to become a base stealer must realize the great deal of study and hours of practice necessary.

An athlete should work to have an initial success rate stealing of above 80 percent. If the athlete studies pitchers' movements, learns to vary his leads, and understands he should continue with the steal when the jump is there but shut it down when it is not, his success rate will probably increase to the 90 percent range.

A base stealer should feel as comfortable off the base as when standing on it. An opposing pitcher or coach can read immediately when a player takes a lead whether the athlete is relaxed and has plans to steal.

A dominating base stealer who puts pressure on the defense as soon as he steps off the base will sometimes turn the game away from home plate and toward him. This athlete immediately demonstrates his comfort leading off the base and his ability to act as a decoy, control the tempo of the game, and make the defense worry about him stealing the base. The following section discusses stealing in various situations.

Stealing Second Base

The base runner must know where the ball is before stepping off any base. If anyone but the pitcher has the ball, the runner should stay on the base to prevent him from being tagged out on a hidden ball trick.

If the pitcher does not have the ball, he must be off the dirt portion of the mound. Otherwise, the pitcher would be called for a balk and no runner can be tagged out. The base runner should make sure the ball is in the pitcher's hand and the pitcher is on the dirt portion of the mound.

KNOWING AND READING PITCHERS

There is nothing close to a science in knowing and reading pitchers. The base runner's ability and instinct improve with lots of concentrated practice, tremendous attention when others are on base, and experience on the basepath. Plus, mistakes by a base runner are an excellent teacher in the learning process. Even a prepared runner who has seen it all and cataloged pitchers' moves can be surprised. But the base runner who has studied pitchers' tendencies and movements knows what the pitcher is going to do before the pitcher does it. This is just smart baserunning.

When I teach base runners about pitchers, I first talk about runners knowing the patterns of pitchers, both right- and left-handed, and their basic movements. I encourage runners to know these elements better than the pitchers themselves so they almost always know what the pitcher is going to do before the pitcher does. Overall, pitchers are not very "baseball intelligent." They practice moves to the bases very little and take runners on base for granted, acting at times as if they don't exist. Taking all of this into consideration, many more base runners should dominate pitchers and the defense.

Reading Right-Handed Pitchers

Ninety-nine percent of right-handed pitchers do the same thing. They begin by opening their shoulder with their foot on the rubber and, prior to taking the signal, look at the runner's lead. Why do they do this? Brian Roberts' research proves correct that after the runner is off the base about 8 feet (2.4 m) the right-handed pitcher can hardly see him. So the pitcher tries to see the runner's lead before he sets.

At this point, the runner is anticipating the pitcher's movement, but the runner's jump is not dependent on when the pitcher moves. The mistake almost all base runners still make is waiting to make their initial movement until after the pitcher moves.

The runner should concentrate only on a right-handed pitcher's left side. The right side is a nonfactor in reading right-handed pitchers except for the foot stepping off at times. Right-handed pitchers who step off with the right foot usually have no clue how to hold runners on and are just stalling and delaying being run on.

Left-side concentration should be general and not confined to one specific area. The left shoulder, left hip, left knee, and left foot play a part, but none of these areas creates any real concern for a knowledgeable base runner. The runner prepares to make his first movement *prior* to the pitcher moving any part of the left side. Pitchers usually have a one-count pattern, which is to set themselves, count one second, and then either deliver to the plate or toss to first base. The second most popular count is four seconds. Whatever the count, almost all right-handed pitchers today are robotic, simple to read, and slow in their pickoff delivery. If the runner is leaning or has movement into a controlled jump *prior* to the pitcher's movement, the base runner is off to the races from first base as the pitcher's left leg comes up.

One of the ways a pitcher tries to minimize the effectiveness of the base runner is to use a slide step. This means the pitcher is trying to cut down his time to the plate so the catcher has a better chance of throwing out a runner. However, pitchers who use a slide step usually lose some velocity and control, so less than 25 percent of pitchers in baseball use a slide step.

Reading a slide step is easy. If a runner is leaning or taking a controlled jump at first base, he has started the initial controlled movement toward second when the pitcher's leg comes up. The runner continues to keep his eyes on the pitcher's left side for one to three steps. If the runner reads a slide step but has a great jump, he usually will continue the attempted steal. If the runner reads a slide step and did not have an adequate jump, he shuts it down and turns the movement into a secondary lead.

Runners should *never* worry about a right-handed pitcher's movements while trying to hold a runner on first base. There are so few right-handed pitchers who do a decent job of holding runners that a base runner absolutely knows he can read a right-handed pitcher easily. He should use his energy to make sure that once he leaves the base, his anticipation button is on, his movement is prior to the right-handed pitcher's and controlled, and his chest remains parallel to the third-base line for one to three steps. This allows the runner to react well to the pitcher's throw.

Reading Left-Handed Pitchers

Left-handed pitchers have become even more robotic than right-handed pitchers. Few left-handed pitchers work on the three areas of movement with the lead or right leg that would help them develop a tough-to-read move. These movements are lifting the leg straight up, lifting the leg at a 30-degree angle, and lifting the leg at a 45-degree angle. The head goes through several movements with each leg movement. If a runner ever competes against a left-handed pitcher who has mastered these movements, such as Andy Pettitte of the New York Yankees (Pettitte may be the only left-handed pitcher in the major leagues who actually has a nonrobotic move), he most likely will not read or guess but run off the first movement of the pitcher. This means that against leg movements like Pettitte's most runners are gambling when they run on the pitcher's first movement that the pitcher will throw home or make a slower move than usual if throwing to first base. The runner may be able to beat a throw from the first baseman into second.

Most left-handed pitchers lift the lead leg and hold it longer in the air to try to read the runner's movement. Runners want these left-handed pitchers to throw to first base often. The more often they throw, the more reads the runner sees. The runner can turn those reads into steals. These left-handed pitchers do not worry runners, are easy to read, and can be dominated. The runner uses short variable leads with controlled jumps to combat the leg hold in the air by left-handed pitchers.

Left-handed pitchers who use a slide step are easily readable by specifically watching the knee. The knee barely bends and the body leans toward home plate immediately. Usually they use this movement because they do not have a quality full-leg pickoff move.

Runners should pay little attention to the back or left side of a left-handed pitcher on the mound. Some left-handed pitchers step off often with the left foot because they do not have a quality move. As they step off, they use a side-arm flip throw to first base, which often is not very accurate.

The runner's concentration is on the right side of a left-handed pitcher. The shoulder, hip, knee, and foot all come into play, with the knee and foot most important. If the knee or foot ever crosses the plane of the rubber as the leg goes backward with the only runner on first, the pitcher must throw to the plate. This is the reason left-handed pitchers keep the right foot, when picked up in the stretch, in front of the rubber. It helps them delay their commitment to throw either to first base or home plate a fraction longer.

READING CATCHERS

The amateur catcher's game is dominated by pitches and pickoffs called from the dugout. This is one of the worst moves the game of baseball has ever seen. Coaches should prepare players in practice to make their own calls and allow players to play the complete game.

Reading amateur catchers begins with reading the coach's mind in the dugout. This is easier than reading active catchers. Coaches become as habitual as pitchers; they have patterns and try to help their pitchers too much. This slows down the game and takes catchers out of rhythm. Many coaches delay action because they are trying to steal the opposing team's signals before they give their own signal to the catcher from the dugout. Calling pickoffs and pitchouts from the dugout is also happening at the minor and major league level. Professional catchers are consistently looking into the dugout with runners on first base.

Runners should practice keeping the head straight and toward the catcher when leading off at first and allowing their peripheral vision to pick up the pitcher. This focus might allow runners to pick up some pitches called by catchers by noticing their body patterns. For example, the catcher may move his wrists in an odd way on a curve ball. The runner can pick this up, and runners like to run on breaking balls. Another catcher may set his feet in an odd way on a certain pitch or change his depth behind home plate. He may hold the glove in a particular way on certain pitches or may always set up on the outside of the plate on a fastball so his throwing lane is good. A runner should look for these tendencies whether in the dugout or on the bases.

BASE-STEALING LEADS

Leads are discussed in chapter 3. This chapter expands on leads and offers ways to use them to become a more successful base stealer.

Primary or Comfort Zone Lead

The primary or comfort zone lead can be used at any time and at any base. This lead is any comfortable distance a runner can move off the base. Again, a runner should feel as comfortable off the base as he does with his foot on it. This idea led me to coin the term *comfort zone*.

For teaching purposes, I like to use a line at 12 feet (3.7 m) as a marker the left foot should be on or near when a primary or comfort zone lead is complete. However, a primary or comfort zone lead can be at almost any distance.

Variable Lead

A variable lead takes the base stealer off the base from 3 to 12 feet (1-3.7 m). Wherever the left foot ends up planted is the designated distance from the bag. All base stealers should use variable leads more often on pitches, even when they are not running, to generate a better comfort zone more consistently. A runner of average speed may receive the most benefit from varying his leads. It will help the average runner to regularly use leads as decoys and enhance the runner's opportunity to use the controlled jump lead more.

Leaning Lead

A leaning lead can be tried at any footage. The key is for the base stealer to gain just a fraction of momentum from a balanced leaning lead. This may help his jump and improve his success stealing.

The leaning lead can be used against any pitcher at any time. For some base stealers, it becomes their favorite option. However, it does take a great deal of work to polish this skill. The runner needs to use the right leg and foot correctly after he takes his primary or comfort zone lead. The runner comes to a standstill after completing the lead (figure 7.1a). From a balanced athletic stance, his right foot opens a little toward second base and the runner begins to lean out over the right foot (figure 7.1b). The foot should remain at a 45-degree angle and not totally open toward second base. This way the runner can maintain balance and strength over the right ankle, even though the weight is on it, and will be able to return to first base safely on a pickoff attempt because the chest is still mostly parallel to the third-base line. The runner can then push off the right foot and make that explosive crossover step back to first base.

Figure 7.1 Leaning lead: *(a)* The base runner takes his comfort zone lead and stops; *(b)* from a balanced athletic stance, he opens his right foot to a 45-degree angle to second base and leans over the right foot, chest still parallel to the third-base line.

As the pitcher starts moving his hands to come to the set, the runner begins the lean before the pitcher's lead leg comes up. Sometimes with a right-handed pitcher the runner cannot see when the hands are setting, but he must develop a good feel for the timing and make sure he leans as the pitcher's hands come down toward the set. When the runner leans and begins the initial step in the steal just a split second before the pitcher's lead leg comes up, his leaning lead jump gives him a good chance of having a successful steal (see figure 7.2).

Figure 7.2 Leaning lead with successful steal: *(a)* The base runner leans over the right foot; *(b)* the runner takes his initial steal step just before the pitcher raises his lead leg; *(c)* the runner slides safely into second base.

Decoys Used With Leads

Any base stealer can learn to use a decoy in a lead at any footage. A decoy is any movement designed to distract or fool the pitcher or other defensive player. An example is leaning back toward the base with the left shoulder (see figure 7.3), which might make the pitcher or other defensive players think the base runner isn't comfortable taking leads and won't attempt to run with that type of lead or body language. If the runner can cause the pitcher a tiny mental or physical lapse, it may be just enough for a base runner to generate a tremendous jump and a successful steal.

Figure 7.3 Decoy lead. The base runner takes his lead but leans back toward first base with his left shoulder.

Explosive and Controlled Jump Leads

I have taught the jump lead since I learned about leads and jumps at the Kansas City Baseball Academy in the early 1970s. Joe Tanner, who coached at the academy and had more enthusiasm for base stealing than any coach I have ever known, was most likely the person who instilled the term *jump lead* into my mind. Coach Tanner's love of teaching base stealing and the jump lead led me to make this technique the core of my base-stealing instruction for the past 40 years and instilled in me a passion to pass it on. I had the opportunity to teach base-stealing drills almost daily to a lot of incredibly talented athletes at the academy, many of whom had close to world-class speed. U. L. Washington, Sheldon Mallory, Ron Washington (current manager of the Texas Rangers), Dennis Smith, and Mark Williams are just a few of the names. In minor league baseball, these athletes proved they could steal a lot of bases. However, even with these athletes' speed, not all mastered the jump lead. I was convinced and still am today that an athlete who polished the jump lead could steal at almost any time in any league.

I experimented with my college teams through the years but worked the most with my son Brian, who led the American League in stolen bases in 2007, to figure out ways to try to control the pitcher and the defense and turn the focus of the offensive game at times from the hitter to the base stealer. The jump lead became a key part of my instruction.

The jump lead was taught only at second base at the academy, and for many years second base was the only base from which I taught the jump lead. That changed in about 2003 or 2004 when Brian began to use a jump lead at first base after he reached the major leagues with the Orioles. I had never even thought about using a jump lead at first base, so I was amazed that Brian pioneered the first-base jump lead and showed he could use it effectively at the major league level. I asked him to help me learn to execute and teach it. It was wonderful to turn the teaching from dad to son as he taught the old coach a new base-stealing trick. The jump lead at first base has helped take the base-stealing game I teach, one other coaches are now teaching, to a new level. I call the first-base jump lead the controlled jump lead; at second base I call it the explosive jump lead.

It takes a great deal of detailed teaching by the coach and a lot of rapt attention by the athlete to master the jump lead. Interestingly, more baseball players with average speed seem to learn this technique at a proficient and usable game level than athletes who have been blessed with great speed. Even more interesting is that every former hockey player I have coached has gotten this technique more quickly and precisely than athletes who have played only baseball most of their lives. This usually breaks down to which athletes have a respectively high level of baseball (or maybe hockey) instincts.

Athletes who do the jump lead well have quick, athletic feet that work well in unison. In other words, the athlete has two dominant feet instead of one. Perhaps because of all the footwork drills they do on skates, hockey players seem to be able to grasp the jump lead quickly and cohesively.

Base runners who use jump leads are usually extremely comfortable off the base with a primary lead. These runners vary their lead lengths, use decoys, and have the ability to shift their weight back toward second base and forward toward third base rhythmically, depending on what they want the pitcher to read. If the base runner is able to smoothly and effectively use his movements while the pitcher is moving his head and body before the pitch, and times his explosion into a jump lead before the pitcher raises his lead leg, the base runner will easily steal third base.

The base runner uses physical ability, instincts, timing, and most importantly anticipation to make the steal. *Anticipation* is key to the success of a consistent base stealer. Instincts are a huge part of successful steals too, but anticipation trumps instincts. A player must learn to move prior to certain movements by a pitcher. When he does this, it becomes just a kids' game to the base runner because he has a chance to toy with the pitcher and defense.

In pulling off the explosive lead, which is primarily used at second base, the base runner checks the middle infielders prior to leaving the base (figure 7.4). Rarely, if ever, does he peek at the defensive position players again. Other than the base stealer's instincts, the only help he might receive is one or two prepracticed short prompts from the third-base coach. It is actually better for the runner if no prompts are used because a runner having to listen will have slower instincts and movement.

Figure 7.4 Base runner at second checks the middle infielders: *(a)* second baseman; *(b)* shortstop.

The runner's eyes should be focused on the pitcher and he should be ready to move *prior* to certain pitcher movements. The runner prepares to move by using anticipation and his knowledge of the patterns of the pitcher and middle infielders in holding runners.

The runner takes his lead (figure 7.5) *prior* to the pitcher taking the signal from the rubber. Once the pitcher places his foot on the rubber and turns to look at the catcher for the signal, the runner may add an additional foot or two to the initial lead. Again, the footage varies and the proper distances at both second and first base are covered in chapter 3. The runner uses decoys back toward the base, which does take inches from third base away, as well as small jumps toward third base, which increases the lead by several feet and make up for those inches lost.

Figure 7.5   Explosive jump lead: *(a)* The base runner takes his lead *before* the pitcher gets the signal from the catcher; *(b)* still in his comfort zone lead, he takes the jump and *(c)* heads for third; *(d)* he slides safely into third base with the steal.

As the pitcher looks once, twice, or maybe even three times toward second base, a runner learns how to negate every movement the pitcher makes. The runner stays under control and knows his distance from second base and how to gain the footage he needs with a jump lead to ensure he is safe at third.

The base runner learns the precise balanced jump and the minimum distance needed to ensure he is going to be safe. This know-how comes with practice and game experience. When this kicks in, a player knows whether he can sprint toward third base or has to shut down the run and turn the steal into a secondary lead.

The controlled jump (see figure 7.6), primarily used at first base, makes taking leads against both left- and right-handed pitchers more fun and gives more players success at stealing second. The runner uses variable leads with a controlled jump at first base, normally anywhere from 3 to 7 feet (1-2.1 m). When the controlled jump is completed the left foot should still be inside the 12-foot (3.7 m) line, the guideline for practicing primary or comfort zone leads.

Figure 7.6 Controlled jump lead: *(a)* The base runner at first takes a short lead from first, still within his comfort zone lead; *(b)* his controlled jump is a small shuffle 2 to 4 feet (.61-1.2 m) toward second base *prior* to the pitcher's movement; *(c)* when the runner reads the pitcher is going home with the pitch, he turns the controlled jump into a sprint; *(d)* he safely steals second base.

The runner is anticipating a pitcher's movement and goes into a controlled jump, a small shuffle of approximately 2 to 4 feet (.61-1.2 m), *prior* to any movement by the pitcher. If the pitcher were to turn and throw or step off while the runner is moving, the runner could easily return to the base safely because he is under control—chest still parallel to the third-base line, feet apart, and feet within the 12-foot (3.7 m) practice line. The runner has proven he can return head first into the back side of the base safely on any pitcher if he stays under control within that practice line. If the pitcher's leg comes up and the read is that the pitcher is going to home plate, the runner just turns the controlled jump into a sprint and steal attempt.

The 1970s might sound like a long time ago, but at that time the academy was way ahead of the prevailing research and development of base-stealing techniques. Even today, base stealing is down the list of areas athletes want to improve and possibly dominate. Few base stealers today use the jump lead and even fewer use it with great efficiency.

Spotlight: Jump Lead

Brian Roberts of the Orioles is the only major league player who consistently uses the jump lead at first and second base. Mike Trout, Nate McLouth, and Jacoby Ellsbury have all used a controlled jump at least some of the time. All of these major league athletes are excellent base stealers.

LEARNING TO STEAL SECOND

Through my years of experimenting with athletes practicing leads, I began to do a lot more trial-and-error research and development, searching for new ways to help base stealers learn how their bodies moved during their initial steps off the base. Base stealers need lots of repetitions, just as infielders need hundreds of ground balls and hitters need hours of batting practice, to help them improve. During this research, I found I needed to break down at a more in-depth level every movement a runner makes once he leaves the base. My research came down to finding the best way to teach rhythmic body movement once the runner leaves the base: by asking him to close his eyes as he practices taking varying leads.

An athlete who can comfortably take leads with his eyes closed and his head toward the pitcher, stay relaxed and use his feet like a ballet dancer, practice varying leads, and actually hit his marks most of the time will be extremely comfortable with his eyes open. This comfort is critical because many athletes taking a lead from a base and possibly trying to steal rarely look comfortable. Either their lack of repetitions in practice or lack of understanding of their bodies makes them look unnatural and awkward.

To practice, blindfold yourself so you can see zero light from under the blindfold. All is totally dark. Try to walk around your house or apartment. If possible walk around the perimeter of the house or apartment complex with someone beside you for safety. Please do not try this exercise anywhere near a street. Even when you are familiar with the architecture and surroundings of your residence, it is difficult to feel comfortable where you are stepping. Imagine what it would be like to be in a strange residence or building if you could not see where you were stepping.

When a runner leaves first base to set up a possible steal of second, he should have practiced his leads so much that his mind is at ease and his body has an innate sense of exactly where each foot should go for each lead. This comfort zone helps the base stealer turn his concentration and anticipation on the steal itself and off his location away from the base.

A base stealer should know each movement his body is about to make so the body can repeat the movement on any lead with comfort and confidence. The athlete should have the upper body aligned properly with the third-base line to be able to make quick sprinter-like turns to the left and right (see figure 7.7). The lower body, especially the feet, should be able to take similar steps each time the runner sets up, whether taking a primary or short and varied lead.

Figure 7.7   Runner's upper body is aligned with the third-base line.

FOOTAGE OF LEADS FROM FIRST BASE

As a runner leaves first base, he should always know the size of the lead—be it 3, 6, 9, or 12 feet (1, 1.8, 2.7, and 3.7 m) or somewhere in between. Knowing the footage makes the runner comfortable with the movement needed and the time it will take to get back to the base on a pickoff move or get to second base. A runner who takes a 6-foot (1.8 m) lead can fall on top of first base easily to return safely but better have a heck of a jump to have any chance of stealing second. Knowing the footage is a big key to polished and consistent movement in either direction.

A SPRINTER'S STANCE

Beginning the process of stealing second base starts with a comfortable lead, a relaxed body off the base, and the rhythmic ability to return smoothly to the base or make an explosive start toward second. Runners should learn to set up in a balanced athletic stance, arms relaxed and hands hanging just above the knees, chest facing the third-base line, feet approximately shoulder-width apart, and toes lined up evenly (see figure 7.8). The stance is balanced and strong, similar to a basketball player preparing to shoot a free throw with both feet almost touching the foul line; a football linebacker waiting for the snap of the ball; or a hockey goalie preparing for a skater with the puck coming right down the center of the ice. The athlete is prepared to move in either direction.

Figure 7.8 Base runner taking a lead with a balanced, athletic stance.

When a runner is returning to first, the athlete should move from a balanced stance as he rotates toward first base to a sprinter's stance before extending his arms to dive back to the base (see figure 7.9). The left arm rotates powerfully to the left side so the hand ends up alongside the hip. The right arm rotates out in front of the body so the hand is beginning to extend toward the base. The left foot, which is nearest the base, pivots. The athlete should keep the left toes closed just a fraction to keep the left side strong and balanced instead of rotating the foot totally open. The right foot rotates fully open so the toes face the base after rotation. Once the runner has rotated as if returning to the base, he is in a sprinter's stance, although without his hands on the ground.

Figure 7.9 Base runner rotating to go back to first: *(a)* The left arm rotates to the left side and the left hand ends near the hip as the left foot pivots while the right arm rotates in front of the body and the right hand extends toward first base as the right foot rotates toward first base; *(b)* the base runner dives back to first base.

When a base stealer is turning to the right to steal second base, the right arm rotates powerfully to the right side so the hand ends up alongside the hip, and the left arm rotates out in front of the body as if the hand is extending toward second base (see figure 7.10). The right foot, which is nearest second base, pivots. The athlete should keep the right toes closed just a fraction to keep the right side strong and balanced instead of rotating the foot totally open. The left foot rotates fully open so the toes face second base after the rotation. Once the runner rotates as if stealing second base, he is in a sprinter's stance, although without his hands on the ground.

Figure 7.10 Base runner rotating to steal second: *(a)* The right arm rotates to the right side and the right hand ends near the hip as the right foot pivots while the left arm rotates in front of the body and the left hand extends toward second base as the left foot rotates toward second base; *(b)* the base runner starts for second.

LEANING OVER THE LEAD FOOT

A base stealer needs to rotate the body efficiently when moving in either direction and gradually lean out over the top of the lead foot. The lead foot should stay in contact with the ground as the body rotates to help with quick acceleration and power.

Many athletes either pick up and retract the lead foot, which costs the runner time, distance, and power, or take a short jab step, which means the first stride is very short. Runners should strive for a low, long, and strong initial stride.

ANTICIPATING THE PITCHER'S ACTION

No matter the style or distance of the lead a runner takes at first base, *anticipation* is the most important factor when trying to steal second. The runner must anticipate the pitcher's actions and move before the pitcher. Potential base stealers who have not worked on anticipation wait for the pitcher to move first. This is too late to allow a base stealer consistent jumps, and it decreases his chances of being safe.

When preparing to steal, the base stealer's mind goes to work before his body. The runner should train himself to make some kind of controlled movement before the pitcher makes any movement to throw to first base or home plate. The runner knows how and when a pitcher will start his movement. The base runner can use this information to move before the pitcher.

When an athlete leaves first base he should immediately anticipate the first movement by the pitcher. The athlete focuses on the home plate side of the pitcher's body and worries little about the foot on the rubber stepping off to become an infielder throwing an attempted pickoff.

When to move is critical. As the runner takes his lead, no matter the distance, he is planning to make his initial move to steal before any movement by the pitcher. The runner's movement is under control but begins to fire the legs and glutes to explode into the sprinter's stance, which then propels the athlete toward second base.

Many base runners trying to become base stealers have no movement prior to the pitcher moving. This is certainly okay, and this technique is used by most baseball players today. If a base runner is most comfortable with not moving before the pitcher throws, he should still be anticipating when the pitcher will start his movement. A dead mind and body prior to an attempted steal means a low success rate.

A runner who starts flat-footed still needs to understand when his jump is good and when he moved late. Runners who go from a standstill have to stop an attempted steal more often because of the difficulty of getting a good jump from a stationary position. The distance for a standstill lead should be 10 to 12 feet (3 to 3.7 m) with the left foot on the imaginary practice line. Any lead less than this distance makes a successful steal very difficult.

But why wait for the pitcher when the athlete can begin moving before the pitcher? Athletes who want to become base stealers should experiment with many methods to get the best jump possible to steal second base.

STEALING SECOND BASE WITH A LEANING PRIMARY LEAD

The leaning lead is the initial way in which I teach athletes to anticipate any movement by the pitcher. The leaning lead starts the process of movement and gets the athlete thinking like a base stealer. The footage for a leaning lead is somewhere from 9 to 12 feet (2.7-3.7 m) off the base (see figure 7.11), with the left foot on that imaginary line.

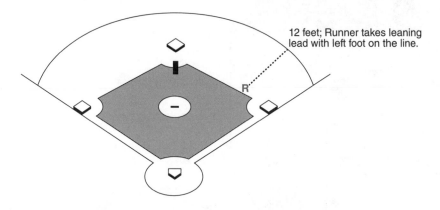

12 feet; Runner takes leaning lead with left foot on the line.

Figure 7.11 Distance for the leaning lead from first base.

The athlete takes a primary lead, no matter the distance, and anticipates the pitcher's initial movement. Prior to that movement the base stealer is leaning at approximately a 45-degree angle out over his right leg (see figure 7.12). The right knee bends over the top of the right foot. The chest remains parallel to the third-base line so if the pitcher turns and throws to first base, the runner can easily return to the bag safely.

Figure 7.12 Base runner leaning over his right leg prior to starting his stealing movement.

The runner is focusing on the home plate side of the pitcher, anticipating that his leg will come up as he delivers to home plate. The athlete is always thinking, "I want to go right," even though the body must stay in control to be able to move back to the base easily and safely.

As the athlete begins his movement over the right leg, he is in an elongated sprinter's stance as he makes the turn. The first two or three steps should be long and low, and the body gradually comes up during the spring phase of the steal (see figure 7.13).

Figure 7.13 Beginning the steal with a leaning primary lead: (a) elongated sprinter's stance over the right leg; (b) first steps are long and low; (c) body comes up during the spring phase of the steal.

STEALING SECOND BASE WITH A CONTROLLED JUMP LEAD

Brian Roberts had used a very aggressive jump lead at second base since he was in middle school but had never tried a jump movement at first. The movement had to be toned down to a controlled jump lead at first base and Brian had to spend many hours practicing to find the best distance off the base to begin a controlled jump lead and still be able to return to first base safely if the pitcher decided to throw over.

This experimentation came about due to Brian being the only base stealer on the Orioles for several years. Pitchers began slide stepping when he was on base a majority of the time to try to stop him from running. His goal was to find a way to have a controlled jump start *prior* to any movement by the pitcher and negate the additional time picked up by the pitcher using a very short or slide leg kick to the plate. Again, a base runner has to anticipate the pitcher's movement so the runner can move before the pitcher and have the advantage.

The controlled jump lead is shorter than either a regular or leaning primary lead, usually no more than 8 feet (2.4 m) from the base. The key here is not the initial distance of the lead but the timing of the jump *prior* to the pitcher's movement and the total distance from the base once the jump lead is completed.

The athlete takes a 6-foot (1.8 m) lead with his left foot (see figure 7.14a), anticipating when the pitcher will make his first movement, regardless of direction. Prior to the pitcher's movement, the runner takes a 3- to 6-foot (1-1.8 m) controlled jump lead (see figure 7.14b). The movement is very similar to a short and controlled secondary lead after the pitch is made.

After a lead that places the left foot on that 6-foot (1.8 m) imaginary line, the runner then takes a small controlled jump prior to the pitcher moving, leaving his left foot on the 10-foot (3 m) imaginary line. This footage still allows the runner to easily return to the base safely if the pitcher makes a move to first.

During the controlled jump, the chest stays parallel to the third-base line. The feet shuffle softly aligned toward home plate. The entire body stays relaxed and moves in a fluid motion toward second base.

Once the base runner is moving, he concentrates to see if the side of the pitcher's body nearest home plate begins to move. If the pitcher's leg comes up and continues to home plate, the runner's right foot lands and he sprints toward second base (see figure 7.14, c and d). The runner has timed the jump perfectly and should have tremendous momentum toward stealing the base.

Figure 7.14   Beginning the steal with a controlled jump lead: *(a)* Initial primary lead; *(b)* controlled jump; *(c)* base runner's right foot lands; *(d)* base runner begins sprint to second base.

If the pitcher turns to throw to first base during the controlled jump lead, the runner pushes off the landing or right leg, takes a step, and dives back into the base safely (see figure 7.15). This ability to get back to the base is the primary reason to use a controlled jump and not an explosive jump, as practiced at second base when working to steal third.

Figure 7.15 Return to first base after a controlled jump lead: *(a)* Base runner takes jump lead; *(b)* base runner pushes off his landing leg; *(c)* he steps and dives back to first base safely.

What the Pitcher Sees From the Mound

When Brian was researching the controlled jump lead at first base, he learned that beyond the 8-foot (2.4 m) lead area off first base, the right-handed pitcher rarely saw any movement. Once Brian had this information, he felt even more comfortable leaning and jumping before the pitcher moved. He learned that a base stealer could gain momentum toward second base before the right-handed pitcher realized he was moving.

As his confidence for anticipating and moving early versus a right-handed pitcher developed, Brian began to use this movement in front of left-handed pitchers. He was trying to get into the left-handed pitcher's psyche to see if he could get him to make a mistake and also to see if he could gain ground even when the pitcher was facing the runner.

During the past several seasons, I have experimented with having my college team's base runners face right-handed pitchers. I confirmed that many right-handed pitchers do not see movement beyond 8 feet (2.4 m), and now I teach the jump lead at first base to all my athletes. I teach the jump lead versus left-handed pitchers as well but have runners start with a shorter lead before going into the jump.

SPRINTING TO SECOND BASE

In part IV, Tim Bishop writes about speed and quickness and focuses on stride length and frequency. Stride length is the distance of ground covered by each stride. Stride frequency is the number of cycles or turns covered in a given distance.

An athlete should practice coming out of the sprinter's stance efficiently and gradually lifting the height of the body. Then the athlete practices stride length to cover more ground in each stride. The next step is for the athlete to practice turning the strides over as fast and efficiently as possible in a direct line to the final destination. As the athlete practices the sprint portion of the steal, he becomes more rhythmic and through better rhythm improves speed.

SLIDING INTO SECOND BASE

Chapter 2 covers how to slide efficiently, an area baseball players tend to practice the least. When a base stealer realizes that he and the ball are likely going to arrive at second base at almost the same moment, he needs to know the best way to place part of his body on the base at the earliest possible moment during the slide and also how to avoid a tag.

Most base stealers have a preferred slide. Immediately after leaving a base to attempt a steal, they know almost 100 percent of the time if they are sliding feet or head first. Even though some runners look back at the catcher for a split second each time they try to steal, their primary focus early in the run is on how the infielder approaches the base and to which side he sets up. If this can be read soon enough the runner can sometimes move to one side or the other, but this is difficult to do in such a short distance. Most of the time the runner has a part of the base he likes to touch first, whether with the foot or hand.

Spotlight: Sliding Into Second

Here are two examples of a player's preferred slide. Carl Crawford likes to slide feet first on his left side when he comes into second base and tries to touch the first-base side of second with the side of his right foot directly in the middle of the base. Brian Roberts usually slides head first to the outfield side of second base, touches the nearest corner with his left hand, continues the slide past the base, and finishes by catching the nearest corner with his left foot as the left hand comes off.

If a player wants to know exactly where he will touch the base each time and also have a chance of avoiding a tag because he can change the placement of his hand, then Brian's slide is the choice. If a player wants an easier slide to perfect and likes to go into the middle of a base, then Carl Crawford's slide is for him.

Stealing Second Base

OBJECTIVES

Practice anticipation, variable leads, ways to pick up momentum, and sprinting and sliding into second base.

EQUIPMENT

A clear area to take leads from a base or a field to make a complete steal.

EXECUTION

The best setup to practice stealing second base is to have a runner at first base, a pitcher on the mound, a first baseman holding the runner, a catcher behind the plate, and middle infielders covering second base to take the throw. Use live action, with the pitcher working to hold the runner on and improve his throw time to the plate. The catcher works on throws to second base. The infielders move to practice setting up at the bag and tagging the runner. The base stealer works on anticipation, varying leads, jumps, the sprint position, sprinting, and sliding.

COACHING POINTS

This is a game situation. The base runner must know where the ball is before leading off the base. The runner anticipates the pitcher's movement and practices varying leads. The runner also works on the following: the sprint position, both to the right and left; the slide back to the base from varying distances using multiple leads; and the initial steps into the sprint and slide into second.

Stealing Third Base

Once a runner arrives at second base, he has a freedom not available at first or third. Even though a throw from the pitcher to second base reaches the defensive player in about the same amount of time it takes to make a throw to the other bases, the runner knows the middle infielders play farther away from the base than on the corners of the infield. This additional space frees the runner's mind and relaxes him. Base runners take advantage of this space to saunter off the base more comfortably, take a walking lead, jump around, maybe dance away from the base, and just play with the pitcher more. For a runner, this freedom and space are a 90-foot (24.7 m) piece of base-stealing heaven.

KNOWING AND READING PITCHERS FROM SECOND BASE

There is nothing close to a science in knowing and reading pitchers. The base runner's ability and instinct improve with lots of concentrated practice, tremendous attention when others are on base, and experience on the basepath. Plus, mistakes by a base runner are an excellent teacher in the learning process. Even a prepared runner who has seen it all and cataloged pitchers' moves can be surprised. But the base runner who has studied pitchers' tendencies and movements knows what the pitcher is going to do before the pitcher does it. This is just smart baserunning.

When I teach base runners about pitchers, I first talk about runners knowing the patterns of pitchers, both right- and left-handed, and their basic movements. I encourage runners to know these elements better than the pitchers themselves so they almost always know what the pitcher is going to do before the pitcher does. Overall, pitchers are not very "baseball intelligent." They practice moves to the bases very little and take runners on base for granted, acting at times as if they don't exist. Taking all of this into consideration, many more base runners should dominate pitchers and the defense.

Ninety-nine percent of pitchers have essentially the same rhythm or pattern with runners leading off second base. The pitcher is on the back or side of the dirt portion of the mound between pitches and takes a quick glance at the runner. He then straddles the rubber and looks back quickly at the runner. With this peek at the runner, few pitchers get an accurate read of the runner's footage off the base. Finally, the pitcher places his back foot (pivot foot) on the rubber and turns his head to the catcher to pick up the signal.

Runners' footage will vary, but much more important than footage is that runners have turned on the anticipation button and are concentrating on being slightly ahead of the pitcher's first movement after the catcher gives the signals. Runners' leads and jumps do not depend on when the pitcher moves. Most base runners still make the mistake of waiting to move until after the pitcher moves.

Once the pitcher has the signal, his first significant movement is almost always with the head. The runner should anticipate a pitcher's head moving after the signal is taken and should have begun to move before the pitcher moves his head.

Pitchers usually have a pattern of one or two looks at the runner before delivering to home plate. If the runner has practiced watching a pitcher's head, the number of turns toward second base by the pitcher should not bother him and in fact should actually help him improve his rhythm with leads and jumps at second base. Whatever the number of head turns, pitchers are robotic, easy to read, and slow in lifting the lead leg to deliver the ball to home plate or second base.

It is rare that a pitcher will use a slide step when pitching with a runner on second base. Most pitchers prefer to use their normal leg kick. If a pitcher is using a slide step with a runner on second base, it is normally because he uses this step at all times from the stretch.

The next body movement a base runner learns to read is a pitcher lifting his front or lead leg. When the pitcher lifts the lead leg, the runner must learn to read whether the knee is turning back toward second base, toward an inside move, or toward the plate for the throw home.

When a pitcher turns to fake a throw or throw to second base, it is usually an extremely slow and robotic move. Many times the pitcher actually has no interest in throwing, and there is no defensive player near the base to catch the baseball from the pitcher.

When a pitcher is definitely throwing home, the base runner should have picked this up early due to the pitcher's robotic head movement toward home plate and leg pickup after his eyes see the target. Very few pitchers pick the leg up while looking at second base. A base runner can use this time to take a tremendous jump, which leads to great success stealing third base.

READING CATCHERS

The amateur catcher's game is dominated by pitches and pickoffs called from the dugout. This is one of the worst moves the game of baseball has ever seen. Coaches should prepare players in practice to make their own calls and allow players to play the complete game.

Reading amateur catchers begins with reading the coach's mind in the dugout. This is easier than reading active catchers. Coaches become as habitual as pitchers; they have patterns and try to help their pitchers too much. This slows down the game and takes catchers out of rhythm. Many coaches delay action because they are trying to steal the opposing team's signals before they give their own signal to the catcher from the dugout. Calling pickoffs and pitchouts from the dugout is also happening at the minor and major league level. Professional catchers are consistently looking into the dugout with runners on first or second base.

Runners should practice keeping the head straight and toward the catcher when leading off at first and allowing their peripheral vision to pick up the pitcher. This focus might allow runners to pick up some pitches called by catchers by noticing their body patterns. Catchers normally use multiple signals with a runner on second base. The runner looks for patterns or giveaways that may help him pick up a called pickoff or a breaking ball, which is an excellent pitch to steal on. Some catchers may set their feet in an odd way on a certain pitch call or change their depth behind home plate. They may hold their glove in a particular way on certain pitches and may set up on the outside of the plate on a fastball so their throwing lane is good. A runner should look for these tendencies whether in the dugout or on the bases.

LEADS AT SECOND BASE

Primary or comfort zone leads vary greatly at second base. The average lead taken at second base is directly in line with third base, with the left foot on the imaginary practice line approximately 15 feet (4.6 m) from the base. Since the second baseman and shortstop normally set up defensively farther away than this, most base runners feel comfortable in this area. I teach an 18- to 21-foot (5.5-6.4 m) lead, discussed later in this chapter.

Nonstealing primary or comfort zone leads are usually at a 45-degree angle from second base and toward a deep shortstop position. The left foot is again on an imaginary line approximately 12 feet (3.7 m) from second base, which matches the distance of the primary lead at first. If the base runner has to return to second on a throw, he can use the same technique used at first base. When a base runner knows he is not working to steal third base, this lead is comfortable yet aggressive and gives the runner a good view of where the second baseman and shortstop are playing.

LEARNING TO STEAL THIRD

Initial leads at second base are much more relaxed than those at first. At second base, if the athlete knows the pitcher has the ball on the dirt portion of the mound, he can take a comfortable lead toward third. Since the defensive player does not stand at the bag like at first base, the base runner has much more freedom to maneuver off the base safely. Once the base runner finds his initial lead, the physical setup is identical to that at first base. The chest is parallel to the first-base line and the feet are shoulder-width apart with the toes about even on the dirt (see figure 8.1).

Figure 8.1   Base runner at second base set up in his initial lead.

ANTICIPATING THE PITCHER'S ACTION

No matter the style or distance of a runner's lead off second base, *anticipation* is the first and most important aspect of trying to steal third or any base. The runner must anticipate the pitcher's action and move before he does. Potential base stealers who have not worked on anticipation still wait for the pitcher to move first. This is too late to allow consistent jumps and increase the chances of being safe.

When preparing to steal, the base stealer's mind goes to work before his body. The runner should train himself to make some kind of controlled movement before the pitcher makes any movement to throw to first base or home plate. The runner knows how and when a pitcher will start his movement. The base runner can use this information to move before the pitcher.

When an athlete leaves second base, he should immediately anticipate the first movement by the pitcher. At second base, the base runner should read the movement of the pitcher's head back and forth in the pitcher's initial movement.

When to move is critical. As the runner takes his lead, no matter the distance, he is planning to make his initial move to steal before any movement by the pitcher. The runner's movement is under control but begins to fire the legs and glutes to explode into the jump lead, which then propels the athlete toward third base.

Many base runners trying to become base stealers have no movement prior to the pitcher moving. This is certainly okay, and this technique is used by most baseball players today. If a base runner is most comfortable with not moving before the pitcher throws, he should still be anticipating when the pitcher will start his movement. A dead mind and body prior to an attempted steal means a low success rate.

A runner who starts flat-footed still needs to understand when his jump is good and when he moved late. Runners who go from a standstill have to stop an attempted steal more often because of the difficulty of getting a good jump from a stationary position. The left foot should be on an imaginary line approximately 21 feet (6.4 m) from second base for a standstill lead at second. Any lead less than this distance makes a successful steal very difficult.

But why wait for the pitcher when the athlete can begin moving before the pitcher? Athletes who want to become base stealers should experiment with many methods to get the best jump possible to steal third base.

STEALING THIRD BASE WITH A PRIMARY WALKING LEAD

The walking lead (see figure 8.2) is the initial steps a base stealer takes while anticipating the pitcher's movement, intended to generate nerve activation. Nerve activation is a quiet but powerful force that notifies the body to be ready to explode.

Figure 8.2 Base runner taking a walking lead from second base.

The athlete takes a primary lead from 15 to 21 feet (4.6-6.4 m) and anticipates the pitcher's initial movement. Before the pitcher moves, the athlete begins to casually walk toward third base, keeping good balance so he can move either way (see figure 8.3). The perfect time for the base runner to try to turn the walk into a sprint is when the pitcher turns his head back toward the catcher and raises his lead leg.

The mechanics of the walking lead are similar to those of the secondary lead at first base. The runner must keep his chest almost parallel to the first-base line to aid his peripheral vision. However, an experienced base stealer rarely uses his eyes to know if a middle infielder is pinching the middle for a possible throw from the pitcher. A base runner is better off using instincts honed from a great deal of practice. The runner relies on hearing or simply feeling the movement of the infielders.

Figure 8.3 Base runner at second in his primary lead, body balanced.

JUMP LEAD AT SECOND BASE

The most aggressive approach to stealing third base comes from the jump lead, which can be explosive or modified to resemble the controlled jump lead at first base. However, the jump lead at second must gain more ground than that used at first base due to the catcher's much shorter throw to third.

The explosive jump lead (see figure 8.4) helps players determine if they can improve their base stealing by using a running start instead of a stationary or walking lead. Many athletes who master the jump lead are suddenly more instinctual, which is extremely important to a base stealer's success.

Figure 8.4 Base runner at second base taking an explosive jump lead.

Once a base runner knows the pitcher has the ball on the dirt portion of the mound and where the middle infielders are playing, he is ready to take his initial lead. The initial lead should be a minimum of 15 feet (4.6 m) but preferably closer to 17 or 18 feet (5.2-5.5 m), with the left foot on an imaginary line at or near one of these distances. This distance helps make the jump lead more effective for the runner trying to steal third. The jump lead can be nearly unstoppable when base stealers perfect the timing and distance of their movement off the base.

The runner should take five or six full steps (about 3 ft. or 1 m each) off the base directly toward third in a relaxed and casual approach before the pitcher takes the signal and puts his foot on the rubber. Once the athlete has reached the suggested distance, he focuses on the pitcher. The pitcher is straddling the rubber, getting ready to place his foot down to take the signal. As the pitcher takes the signal from the catcher and his head is facing home plate, the runner should work to casually meander another 2 to 3 feet (.61-1 m) closer to third base. Most of the time the middle infielders are focusing on the catcher's signals so they are paying little, if any, attention to the base runner increasing his lead.

The pitcher takes the sign from the catcher and begins to move his head, hands, feet, and arms to complete the start-up phase of the stretch. Now the runner narrows his focus to the pitcher's head. The pitcher normally looks at the runner in one of three ways.

First, the pitcher might set with his head turned to the catcher. The pitcher's head begins a level turn with the eyes rotating by third (right-handed pitcher) or first base (left-handed pitcher). Then the pitcher's eyes pick up the runner.

Second, the pitcher might set with his head turned to the runner. This means that as the pitcher's arms and feet begin to move after the signal, his head makes the level turn simultaneously.

Third, the pitcher might set with his head facing third (right-handed pitcher) or first base (left-handed pitcher). The pitcher may stay with his head turned to the bag to try to pick up the runner, he may indicate that he sees the runner, or he may turn back to second base or home plate. Some pitchers pick up their leg while their head is facing the bag as well.

Anticipation is key for the base runner as the pitcher takes the signal. It helps ensure that the base runner's mind and body are prepared to move before the pitcher does. The base runner anticipates what the pitcher's head will do and moves into the decoy position.

USING THE DECOY POSITION

The base runner's decoy position is to lean to the left side with the shoulder, knee, head, or entire body (see figure 8.5). When the pitcher sees this position, he thinks the base runner is scared, off-balance, or does not want to be very far from second base and certainly is in no position to execute a great jump to steal third.

Figure 8.5 Base runner's decoy position.

The base runner is now approximately 18 to 21 feet (5.5-6.4 m) off the base. The pitcher has almost completed a signal position on the mound. The runner anticipates that the pitcher will move after the signal is completed, and the base runner switches from a comfortable athletic position in the base line to a decoy position.

As the pitcher's head moves in one of the three patterns discussed earlier to look at the runner at second base, the runner has already anticipated and beaten the pitcher's head turn to make sure he is in the decoy position when the pitcher's eyes first view the runner. The runner shifts his weight to the left side or takes a 4- to 6-inch (10.2-15.2 cm) jab step back toward second base with the left foot. The runner loses a small amount of ground but nothing significant enough to take away the steal of third.

Right after the runner's weight shifts to the left, which fires up the left leg and especially the left glute, the runner springs back toward the right side. There is no hesitation in the mind or body, no sitting on the left side, just a rhythmic movement as the weight starts in the center, moves to the left, and then immediately moves back to the right side.

The pitcher may still be looking at the base runner as the runner begins the slightest movement back toward the right side. This timing is ideal for the base runner. If the base runner waits until the pitcher's head and eyes are rotating back past third base and picking up the target at home plate, the initial part of the jump lead will be too late. As the base runner begins the jump in an elongated shuffle movement to the right, the runner takes a short jab step with and springs off the right foot into a small or exaggerated jump lead (see figure 8.6) anywhere from 4 to 10 feet (1.2-3 m) to as far as 30 feet (9.1 m) from second base.

Figure 8.6 Exaggerated jump lead from second base.

Many base stealers are uncomfortable with a lead of close to 30 feet (9.1 m). This is understandable. In this case, until the athlete becomes more comfortable with the jump lead, he should shorten his primary or comfort zone lead to about 15 feet (4.6 m). This distance can still work for a base stealer but leaves little margin for error in perfectly hitting the first steps of the sprint when the pitcher's leg is just coming up to throw home with the pitch.

Players can practice the jump lead almost anywhere they have 10 to 20 feet (3-6.1 m) of safe space. Set up two parallel lines approximately 10 to 12 feet (3-3.7 m) apart. In the drill, the runner tries to make a rhythmic leap from one line to the other. When leaping to the right, the runner takes a short jab step with his right foot and leaps with his left knee moving up in the air as it crosses over the right leg. The feet should land in the vicinity of the imaginary line 10 to 12 feet away, with the body still parallel to the first-base line, if the drill is performed between second and third base on a baseball field. Next, the athlete immediately takes a short jab step with the left foot and takes the right knee up in the air as it crosses over the left leg and the athlete lands back near the line he just left.

The athlete should practice leaping back and forth several times. During my years of teaching and watching this drill, I have found that few athletes are able to use their right and left feet equally well in sync, at least at first. Every athlete has a dominant foot, but few seem to know which foot it is until beginning the drill. The leaping drill to the right and left is designed to help each foot work equally well and give runners explosiveness in the legs when the glute is fired for the leap.

Jump Lead Drill

OBJECTIVES

Learn to use the feet equally well in moving to the left or right. Learn which foot is dominant and try to bring the other foot up to that strength and maneuverability. Also learn how to gain a lot of ground with the leap.

EQUIPMENT

None.

EXECUTION

Draw two parallel lines on the ground 10 to 12 feet (3-3.7 m) apart. The athlete places his left foot on a line and leaps to or beyond the line to his right. A coach can help by saying, "Right foot out and leap" as the athlete leaps to his right and "Left foot out and leap" as the athlete leaps back to the starting point. The athlete can also say this to himself. Repeat the leap back and forth.

COACHING POINTS

Learn to use both feet equally well. Improve rhythm during practice.

TIMING THE JUMP LEAD

A runner should work on the timing of the jump lead as often as possible. If a coach, teammate, parent, or friend takes the pitcher role and uses a rhythm pattern of one and two looks back to second base, with no deviations, the base runner will be able to improve his timing of the decoy movement, his leaps right and left, and his ability to turn the leap into a sprint for a potential steal. The person acting as a pitcher can mix in one inside move approximately every 10 practice motions. This helps the runner stay under some control and makes sure he is keeping his eyes and chest toward the pitcher until the pitcher's lead leg commits to go to the plate.

A runner should try the jump lead often at second base but definitely not pitch after pitch. A runner needs to be coy with leads and jumps. When a runner tries to hit a jump lead perfectly pitch after pitch, the defense will eventually close ranks on the runner and use more pickoff plays. The base runner should always vary the leads, decoys, and looks he shows to the defense, just as the pitcher tries to vary his looks and timing to shut down the running game. A quality base stealer should always be able to get inside a pitcher's head and turn the game toward the bases. As an athlete becomes a proficient base stealer, he will control a pitcher and possibly the game.

MOVING FROM THE JUMP LEAD TO THE SPRINT

Once an athlete improves the rhythm of the back-and-forth leap and each foot moves well independently, he can practice turning the leap toward third base into a sprint. The following pattern should be followed: right foot out, leap; left foot out, leap; right foot out, leap; left foot out, leap; and on the fifth jump, turn the jump lead to the right into a full sprint.

As the athlete turns the jump lead into a sprint, his head should focus on the center of the pitcher's body. The pitcher's knee will come up, whether he is going to the plate or making a turn toward second base. The pitcher's knee kick can be read well only if the base runner's chest is still parallel to the first-base line.

Reading the pitcher, knowing how he maneuvers while on the mound in the stretch position is key. When a runner practices reading the pitcher's body and leg movements while working on his jump lead at second base, he has more success with the steal.

The runner should never guess what the pitcher will do. Guessing leads to a runner getting caught in the middle between second and third base when a pitcher uses an inside move. The inside move should rarely, if ever, be a threat to stealing third base. During my years of teaching the jump lead at second base, I have seen the pitcher use the inside move hundreds of times. However, *rarely* is an infielder at second base to catch the throw from the pitcher to make the runner out. Therefore, if the runner is balanced and is reading the pitcher, not guessing, he will put on the brakes, make the pivot, and immediately sprint back toward or all the way to second base. The runner is almost always safe if he makes an immediate decision to sprint back to the base.

WHEN TO CONTINUE
OR SHUT DOWN THE SPRINT

Rarely does a coach want an athlete to think about or analyze the game as he plays. Athletes are better off using their instincts than thinking about what to do as the game unfolds. However, with the jump lead, the athlete will make better progress by using intellect and instincts when it comes to deciding whether to continue with the steal or shut it down.

As an athlete uses anticipation and athleticism with the jump lead, he should become more comfortable—moving rhythmically in either direction, staying balanced, and using his eyes to better read the pitcher's movements. The next step is knowing when to go and when to stay.

A runner should be safe every time he tries to steal third base. Some would call this impossible, and years ago I would have agreed. However, Brian Roberts taught me that it can be done when experience kicks in and good decision making is used on the first or second step of the sprint.

The runner gains confidence until he says to himself, "I hit the footage and timing perfectly, so I will be safe." If the runner has the proper footage with the initial lead, adds the additional distance of the jump lead, and perfectly times his steps into the sprint with the pitcher's leg kick, he will be safe unless he falls down or the umpire makes a poor call. If the runner misses a link in this chain and does not feel like he hit the jump perfectly, then he should shut down the steal, go into an extended secondary lead, and pick up the baseball as it crosses the plate.

chapter

Stealing Home ◆9

Stealing home is probably the most exciting play in baseball, but it's also among the most difficult. The timing of the play must be flawless for it to work, and a runner has to read the pitcher and defense perfectly.

If a pitcher decides to throw from the stretch position with a runner on third base, it's almost impossible to steal home if the runner is the sole base stealer. There is just not enough time, even with a large lead, to beat a throw to the plate once the pitcher begins his motion after coming set in the stretch. However, if there is a runner at first base attempting a steal and the defense decides to make a play on the attempt, the runner on third base has a much better chance of stealing home. Chapter 10 covers the double steal in more detail.

When a pitcher is in the windup position, a runner at third base has a much better opportunity to steal home. If the runner has practiced attaining the minimum footage for success and is comfortable getting there, he is off to a good start. The runner must be casual in his approach down the line and have a good initial burst of speed. His timing must be on the button with the start of the pitcher's hand movement. Now it becomes a race between the runner and the pitcher, testing how quickly the pitcher can deliver the ball accurately to the plate without balking. In most cases it is a bang-bang play when a base runner tries to steal home. Adding to the excitement of this play, often the umpire has a poor view of the slide and tag, so correct calls are not always made.

READING THE PITCHER

When a runner reaches third base, he should immediately turn his attention to the pitcher to see whether the pitcher uses the windup or stretch position when he toes the rubber with his pivot foot. Once again, *anticipation* is the key word.

If the pitcher is going from the windup position, the base runner should be ready to move toward home plate as the pitcher places his foot on the rubber. The runner can take a longer lead, fake the steal of home, or take the fake steal into an attempted steal of home. Reading the pitcher from the windup position is covered in more detail shortly.

The pitcher may step off the rubber without being called for a balk if he has not brought his hands to a set position. For example, a pitcher has the glove on his leg and the ball is behind his back. The pitcher has to bring the ball and glove together in front of his body before it is considered a set. The pitcher can still step off with his pivot foot and fake or actually make a throw to third base even as the hand with the ball comes forward to set. The pitcher also can step off while the hands are set if the pivot foot moves first. If the nonpivot foot moves first, the pitcher is called for a balk. Once the hands move together or the nonpivot foot moves, the pitcher can no longer step off the rubber with his pivot foot without a balk being called.

Reading a pitcher from the stretch at third is similar to when at first base. A right-handed pitcher is facing third base, so the runner must primarily watch the pitcher's front side to make sure the knee turns toward home plate before moving to a secondary lead. A left-handed pitcher has his back to the runner at third base. The runner can take a larger primary or comfort zone lead in this instance and increase that lead as the pitcher's leg comes up for the throw to home plate. A runner versus a left-handed pitcher in this situation should take two to four steps more in his lead than with a right-handed pitcher in the stretch.

READING THE CATCHER

The base runner at third should peek at the catcher and concentrate primarily on the catcher's feet. It is difficult for the runner to pick up any of the catcher's signals to the pitcher, especially with a right-handed hitter at the plate, but the runner may still be able to pick up some clues the catcher's body gives about potential pickoffs or pitchouts. Catchers sometimes place their feet deeper in the catcher's box to free themselves from a right-handed hitter's swing on a pitch if they want to throw to third base behind him. Of course, with a left-handed hitter at the plate, the catcher has a clear view of the runner at third base and may actually move up on the outside of the plate to be one step closer to where he wants to throw.

When the runner on third base turns his head toward the plate as the ball is in flight from the pitcher to the catcher, the runner should pick up the catcher's feet immediately. If the catcher has called a pitchout, the runner will be able to see the catcher's outside foot opposite the hitter move outward early, called a cheating step, so the catcher can receive the ball farther out front but without being hit by the batter's swing. In this case, the runner plants the lead foot, stops, and returns to the base safely.

TAKING THE INITIAL LEAD

When a runner is on third base and the pitcher is throwing from the windup, the runner should take a primary or comfort zone lead where the left foot rests on an imaginary line 12 feet (3.7 m) from the base (see figure 9.1). The chest is parallel to the first-base line. The lead should be taken before the pitcher steps on the rubber to take the signal from the catcher. This lead is the same footage as an initial lead at first base or a nonstealing lead at second base. The runner is able to take one step and dive to a corner of third to return to the base easily on any attempted pickoff play.

Figure 9.1 Initial lead about 12 feet (3.7 m) from third base.

Usually the third baseman plays approximately four steps or 12 feet (3.7 m) from the base, although this varies greatly depending on the hitter and the game situation. If the third baseman happens to be playing farther away than four steps from the bag, the runner should feel comfortable moving down the line to a similar distance from the base. Once the pitcher toes the rubber with his pivot foot, he would have to step back off the rubber and become an infielder before he could throw to third base without balking. In the time it takes for the pitcher to make this movement and the third baseman to approach the bag to make the catch, the runner can easily return to the base safely.

READING THE PITCHER
FROM THE WINDUP POSITION

A base runner has a lot to keep track of when the pitcher throws from the windup position. The runner must study how a pitcher approaches the rubber with his feet, what the pitcher does with his gloved hand and free hand, in which hand the baseball is located if the pitcher's hands are separated, where the pitcher's hands are when his foot hits the top of the rubber, and the pitcher's motion when he starts the windup.

Pitchers differ in how they set their feet on the rubber to take the signal. Years ago, most pitchers set up with the chest directly facing the plate and the pivot foot pointed at the catcher. This was considered the best body mechanics to begin the motion. Today, pitchers set up with the chest and pivot foot facing varying angles. Some pitchers start with their hands together and others with their hands apart. Pitchers with their hands apart may have the ball in the glove or the bare hand.

The pitcher is allowed to step off the rubber with the pivot foot any time before he starts his motion to home plate. The runner should watch the right foot of a right-handed pitcher and the left foot of a left-handed pitcher. If the pitcher steps off with the nonpivot foot, it is considered a balk. Runners should know this rule.

A pitcher may start his motion from the windup position in a number of ways. What constitutes the beginning of the windup? If the hands are together, any movement by the body is the beginning of the windup. A pitcher cannot stop his motion or step off the rubber once his body begins to move with the hands together or it is a balk. The runner anticipates when the pitcher's hands will move and makes sure his walking lead takes him beyond 24 feet (7.3 m) before the pitcher's hands or nonpivot leg begins to move. The runner should start to move a split second before the pitcher does.

If the pitcher's hands begin apart, he is allowed to bring them together. Then the pitcher's actual wind-up officially begins. Before the pitcher's hands come together to set, he can stop the motion or step off the rubber with the pivot foot. Few pitchers stop the arm motion as the hands are coming together because it is easier to just step off with the pivot foot.

Pitchers also show variety in their leg kicks. Some pitchers use a high leg kick, others use little leg kick at all, and the rest fall somewhere in the middle. When the pitcher is in the windup, he is supposed to continue with his normal leg kick. However, often umpires allow the pitcher to alter or shorten the leg kick without calling a balk. Shortening the leg kick helps the pitcher throw the ball to the catcher sooner and gives the defense a better chance to get a runner attempting to steal out. With an altered leg kick allowed, the runner must calculate the additional footage he needs to be successful if the pitcher is going to cut down his leg kick to throw home. This altered leg kick is used for the same reason a pitcher uses a slide step to throw home from the windup with a runner on first base.

WALKING LEAD TO RUN

How do all these pitcher permutations affect the runner's initial and secondary leads as he tries to gain an advantage? How does a runner know when to begin his walk and when to turn the walk into a run down the line? The initial lead is still based on two factors. The runner knows where the third baseman is playing and is gambling that the pitcher most likely is paying little attention to the base runner.

Since the pitcher on the mound has his hands apart, he is allowed initial movement to bring them together. This may be a decoy that makes it hard for some base runners to know when to begin the walking lead and turn the walk into a run.

The runner should begin the walking lead (see figure 9.2) right before the pitcher starts to bring his hands together. This normally slow action benefits the base runner because it gives him more time to walk down the line. However, once the pitcher's hands come together, the pitcher may still step off the rubber and throw to a base. With this possibility, the base runner must know his footage away from the base at all times so he can get back if the pitcher steps off with the pivot foot and turns to throw to the third baseman.

Figure 9.2 Base runner on third base begins his walking lead before the pitcher brings his hands together.

The final element of the walk down the line is deciding when to begin the run if the pitcher's hands come together for what some coaches call a double set. The pitcher can step off the rubber on the second set if he comes to a complete stop. The runner must anticipate when the pitcher is going to start again in the second set. It takes some experience to know how to read this wacky movement. *Anticipation* is still paramount, but gambling plays a role too. Of course, the runner must know his footage as well. If the runner can successfully combine these elements, he may have a chance to be safe at home.

The average time for a pitcher from the stretch to throw home from his initial movement to the baseball hitting the catcher's mitt is approximately 1.25 seconds. When a pitcher uses a slide step, the time is cut down to about 1.10 seconds or even closer to 1 second. This means the runner must go from the end of his walking lead to home plate in almost world-class time to be safe unless the pitcher makes a poor throw.

REACHING THE MINIMUM FOOTAGE TO ATTEMPT THE STEAL OF HOME

After years of watching pitchers live as I coached third base, watching video of pitchers' habits when taking the windup, and paying attention to the leads of runners on third who had no interest in stealing home to see how many steps they took without the pitcher paying close attention to them, I formulated a plan to help runners steal home plate. Through trial and error with my players, I honed techniques designed to allow runners to accomplish this against both right- and left-handed pitchers in the windup.

Lead Versus a Right-Handed Pitcher

With a right-handed pitcher in the windup with his hands together in front of his body, the runner must have an initial lead of 18 to 21 (5.5-6.4 m) feet, six or seven steps from third base. The runner is settled in at this distance—he knows how far from the bag the third baseman is playing and that he is able to return to the bag safely—and can concentrate on the pitcher. The runner begins to casually walk toward home plate and anticipates the pitcher's hand movement. Before the pitcher moves his hands, the runner must continue to walk until he is about 27 to 30 feet (8.2-9.1 m) from the base. From this lead, with explosive first steps and a pitcher who goes through a full leg kick, the runner has an excellent chance to be safe at home.

With a right-handed pitcher in the windup with his hands starting apart, the runner must have an initial lead of 15 to 18 feet (4.6-5.5 m), five or six steps from third base. Again, the runner is settled in at this distance and can concentrate on the pitcher. The runner must anticipate when the pitcher will begin to bring his hands together. As the pitcher does this, the runner starts to walk down the line, watching the pitcher's hands and feet as he walks. This is important since the pitcher is allowed to back off the rubber with his pivot foot any time before he moves after the second set. By the time the pitcher comes to the second set, the runner has gained several more steps down the line to approximately 24 to 27 feet (8.2-9.1 m). The runner must anticipate that the pitcher may continue quickly through the second set instead of coming to a distinct pause. Again, the rule book calls for a complete pause, but many times this does not occur.

The runner has a distinct advantage against pitchers who start with their hands apart because he can continue to walk as the pitcher goes through the double set. Sometimes this can be a little scary for the runner since he is much farther from third base at this point than the third baseman. The runner should start his sprint just before the pitcher moves his hands after the second set (see figure 9.3). If a runner can hit this timing, he has an excellent chance to be safe at home.

Figure 9.3   Base runner at third begins to sprint right before the right-handed pitcher moves his hands after the second set.

Lead Versus a Left-Handed Pitcher

Like right-handed pitchers, left-handed pitchers may start with their hands separated or together, but they set up at different angles. However, the left-handed pitcher may have part of his back to the runner at third base either before or during the windup.

Against a left-handed pitcher in the windup, the runner has some distinct advantages when trying to steal home due to the lefty possibly turning his back to the runner on third base (see figure 9.4). If the left-handed pitcher sets up with his chest directly at the plate, his back and certainly his eyes will be away from the runner for a split second as the pitcher goes through his motions. However, against the left-hander who starts the windup with most of his back turned to third base, the runner should have a much better chance to steal home because of being able to attain a larger initial walking lead.

Figure 9.4   Left-handed pitcher with his back to the base runner at third base.

One of the defensive players may have to alert the pitcher that a runner is trying to steal home because the pitcher cannot see the runner. Sometimes the left-handed pitcher may not be able to cut down his leg kick because he does not realize the runner is going as early as a right-handed pitcher, who can see the runner start down the line.

STEALING HOME WITH RUNNERS ON THIRD AND FIRST

The first priority for the defense is to hold the runner at third when the runner at first tries to steal. Due to this emphasis, the runner at third base must read the defense well, anticipating their movement and throws. Guessing the defense's next move won't do. There is a big difference between guessing and reading the play. Reading the play helps the runner make better decisions. If he tries to guess, the runner at third is bound to make mistakes.

Double steals are covered in detail in chapter 10, but here I do want to lay out what the runner at third base does to steal home with a runner moving from first base. With runners on third and first, several plays allow the runner at third a good opportunity to steal home.

Reaction Versus a Right-Handed Pitcher

When the runner at first base is moving on a delayed steal, the runner at third should watch the catcher's feet to see if a pitchout is on. If the catcher's feet move into the batter's box opposite the hitter (see figure 9.5), this freezes the runner at third base and makes it difficult for him to score, even if the catcher throws to second base. The runner at third base also has to be aware that the catcher is in a good position to throw directly at him to make a pickoff attempt.

If there is no pitchout, the runner can meander down the third-base line but must remain aware that the throw can go to second base, the pitcher, or third base—or the catcher may fake a throw. This is why it is so important to anticipate what the defense might do but even more important to read what actually happens with the baseball.

Figure 9.5   If the base runner at third sees the catcher's feet move into the batter's box opposite the hitter, he freezes and watches for the throw.

Anticipating the steal home with runners on third and first should be practiced often since this setup happens many times during the course of a season. The runner at third base should read the throw to have the opportunity to steal home. The only throw that gives the runner at third base the opportunity to steal home is one over the pitcher's mound heading toward second base.

The runner at third base first reads the ball out of the pitcher's hand and then turns his attention to the catcher. Initially the runner reads the catcher's feet. If the catcher stays behind the hitter to catch the baseball and acts like he is making a throw toward second base, the runner should have anticipated this throw, read the flight, and have started controlled steps toward home plate.

As the ball leaves the catcher's hand, the runner reads the angle of the ball toward second base. Is the ball thrown very flat like an old clothes line, or does it arc like a rainbow? If the flight of the ball is very flat, it is more difficult to attain a great jump to steal home. The runner needs to make sure the pitcher does not cut off the ball as it carries past the mound, so this may freeze the runner for a split second. Plus, a low throw usually has great velocity and reaches the shortstop or second baseman quickly, which allows a return throw to the plate sooner if the runner on third attempts to steal home. However, if the flight of the ball arcs, it makes it less challenging to steal home safely. Since the throw is higher and normally of average velocity, the runner is able to get a better jump.

If the runner feels he has a good lead as the ball leaves the catcher's hand in an arc toward second base, he can break for the plate and attempt to steal. The runner should anticipate sliding to the back side of the plate, preferably feet first (see figure 9.6). A runner who decides to slide head first should be sure to go around, not through, the catcher in his attempt to tag home plate.

Figure 9.6 Base runner slides into the back side of home plate feet first.

Reaction Versus a Left-Handed Pitcher

With a left-handed pitcher holding runners at third and first base, the runner at third has a much greater chance of stealing home. Since the left-handed pitcher's back is to the runner on third base, the runner can take a larger initial lead, as much as 18 to 21 feet (5.5-6.4 m). The runner on first base takes a lead or attempts to steal to draw a throw and set up the potential steal of home by the runner on third.

The runner on third anticipates the pitcher's front leg coming up and reads the ball out of the pitcher's hand as he throws to first base. Before the pitcher moves any part of his body, the runner on third walks into a lead that takes him 25 to 28 feet (7.6-8.5 m) from third base. As the pitcher's foot leaves the ground, the runner on third begins to sprint toward home plate. If the pitcher rotates the foot toward home plate and throws to the plate, the runner breaks and busts it back to third base. The lead is so great that the runner cannot stand in the baseline and wait to see if the hitter makes contact because if the ball lands in the catcher's mitt the runner has a decent chance of being picked off if the catcher throws to third. If the pitcher picks up the foot and the throw goes to first base, the runner at third base is already in a dead sprint to the plate (figure 9.7). Sometimes the pitcher will throw the ball on a line to the first baseman, and other times the ball has a rainbow arc. Either way the throw is made, the base stealer at third is in a race with the ball as it is delivered to first base and then thrown to home plate by the first baseman.

The base stealer should plan to go to the back side of the base, preferably feet first. A runner who decides to go head first should go around the catcher and try to tag home plate from the back side to avoid a collision because it's almost always a bang-bang play.

Figure 9.7 Steal of home versus a left-handed pitcher: *(a)* base runner in full sprint from third base; *(b)* base runner goes to the back slide of home plate feet first; *(c)* the base stealer beats the tag by the catcher.

Reading the Ball to Steal Home

OBJECTIVES

Learn to read the ball out of the catcher's and left-handed pitcher's hand.

EQUIPMENT

Baseballs and bases.

EXECUTION

Runners get in position at third and first along with the infield defense. The pitcher throws to home plate, third base, and first base. The catcher is encouraged to make throws to all bases and in some situations go directly back to the pitcher or hold the ball. The runner at first base practices stealing, delayed stealing, fake stealing, and getting caught in a rundown between the bases. The runner at third reads the defense and their throws and learns when to break for home plate.

COACHING POINTS

Base stealers learn to read pitchers and throws. Pitchers learn to hold runners, and the defense learns how to handle the baseball as runners are trying to steal bases.

◇–◇–◇

Double Steal 10

The double steal is a fun play for both runners to learn to execute efficiently. The runners can be at first and second or first and third. Runners should be in synchronization with one another so the attempted steals flow smoothly, similar to the rhythm of a group of rowers or a shortstop and second baseman turning a double play. There should be no guesswork on how to execute. Each runner must know exactly what the other is trying to do when working the double steal in order to react appropriately.

A team baserunning philosophy helps each runner remain comfortable in all situations on the bases and is critical with the double steal due to the pairing of runners of different speeds on the bases. Whether the team has the faster runner on the lead base and the slower runner on the other base, or vice versa, the team should still be able to execute the double steal well if they follow the team baserunning philosophy.

READING THE PITCHER

The pitcher with runners on first and second or first and third, no matter the number of outs, is in a difficult defensive situation. He has to hold the runners and keep them from attempting a double steal. Pitchers in this situation try to concentrate more on getting the next hitter out than they do holding the base runners. So the base runners should try to take advantage and run often in a double-steal setup.

With runners on first and second, the pitcher is primarily paying attention to the runner on second base and rarely attempts a throw to first. Both base runners must anticipate the pitcher's movements. Runners should initially read the pitcher's head movement from the time he looks to the catcher for the signal to when he rotates his head one or more times to the runner on second base. The runners must anticipate that the lead leg may come up at any time through this process for a throw to home plate or second base.

The primary focus for the runner on first base is on his teammate's movement at second so they are in sync on a double steal. The runner on first base should be directly watching his teammate's movement and using his peripheral vision to monitor the pitcher's movements. As the pitcher moves, the runner on first base is also listening for the first-base coach's cue if a blind pickoff attempt is on the way with the first baseman coming in behind the base.

With runners on first and third with either a right- or left-handed pitcher on the mound, the pitcher is primarily paying attention to the runner on first and rarely makes a pickoff attempt to third base in this situation. The runner at first base must anticipate the pitcher's movements. One such move, legal in amateur baseball but illegal in professional baseball, is when a right-handed pitcher picks up his lead leg, steps toward third base, possibly fakes a throw to third, and then turns toward first and possibly makes a throw. This defensive move, actually an attempt to deceive the runner, which is why it is not allowed in professional baseball, forces the runners to hold a split-second longer when attempting a double steal. The runners on both first and third must read that the lead leg is going to the plate before attempting a steal.

With a left-handed pitcher on the mound and runners on first and third, the runners are anticipating the pitcher's movement. Some left-handed pitchers throw to first base often in a first-and-third potential double-steal situation. The runner on first reads the front side of a left-handed pitcher to make sure his leg is going to the plate before attempting a steal. Runners on first base in this situation rarely run off the first movement of the front side of a left-handed pitcher but run off a read of the pitcher's lead leg. The runner on third base is also anticipating the pitcher's movement.

This anticipation and read of the pitcher's front side helps some outstanding base stealers attempt to steal home when the left-handed pitcher throws to first base. Since the left-handed pitcher has his back to the runner on third base, this runner can take a larger than normal lead by walking down the third-base line maybe as far as 30 feet (9.1 m), or approximately 10 steps. As the runner walks and approaches the 30-foot imaginary marker, and the left-handed pitcher's lead leg comes up, the runner turns the walk into a sprint toward home plate. If the pitcher throws to first base, the runner on third base continues to sprint to the plate and tries to steal home. If the pitcher turns the right hip and knee toward the plate and throws home, the runner on third base immediately breaks and sprints back toward the bag.

READING THE CATCHER

With runners at second and first base, the runner at second base has the best opportunity to read the catcher's signals, setup, and body language. The runner at first base should be following the lead of the runner at second and listening to the first-base coach for the potential call of a throw from the catcher. A catcher may give a particular pitch away by the way he gives signals. He may give the location away early by the way he sets his feet. He may give away a potential pickoff from the pitcher to first or second base by his body language or the amount of time it takes him to give the signal. When it takes longer than normal for a pitcher to take a signal and set, that could easily mean a pickoff attempt is coming.

With runners at first and third base, each base runner should be reading the catcher. The runner at first base should be looking for a catcher to give away pitch signs due to variation in his hand or wrist movement on a particular kind of pitch. He should also be watching the catcher's feet as he sets up for a pitch to see if the catcher is trying to create a good throwing lane for a potential steal or setting up away for a called pitchout.

The runner at third base should peek at the catcher and concentrate primarily on the catcher's feet. It is difficult for the runner to pick up any of the catcher's signals to the pitcher on pitches, especially with a right-handed hitter at the plate, but the runner may be able to pick up clues the catcher's body reveals about potential pickoffs or pitchouts. Catchers sometimes place their feet deeper in the catcher's box to free themselves from a right-handed hitter's swing on a pitch if they want to throw to third base behind him. Of course, with a left-handed hitter at the plate the catcher has a clear view of the runner at third base and may actually move up on the outside of the plate to be one step closer to where he wants to throw. When the runner on third base turns his head toward the plate as the ball is in flight from the pitcher to the catcher, the runner once again should pick up the catcher's feet. If the catcher has called a pitchout the runner will be able to see the catcher's outside foot opposite the hitter move outward early, called a cheating step, so the catcher can receive the ball farther out front but without being hit by the batter's swing. In this case, the runner plants the lead foot, stops, and returns to the base safely.

FIRST-AND-SECOND DOUBLE STEAL

The runners on first and second base have equal importance in executing the double steal (see figure 10.1). Some coaches seem to think that the runner on first base is not as important since this runner does not have to run just because the runner on second takes off. However, the runner on first base needs to execute as well as the runner on second. If he practices often, the runner on first will be able to read the runner on second and simultaneously jump to steal.

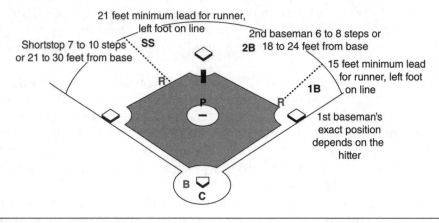

Figure 10.1   First-and-second double steal.

Best Pitch for the Double Steal

The best pitch for stealing a base is the first pitch after a runner arrives on base. This is especially true in a first-and-second double-steal situation. Why the first pitch? In my early years as a head coach, my father would ask me why I liked to run on the first pitch. He'd ask what the difference was between the first pitch and, say, the fourth pitch. This is a legitimate question and one I enjoy answering.

Running on the first pitch has several advantages. First, the pitcher, unless he has an incredibly professional approach, is usually upset or at least bothered by the fact there are runners on first and second base. Maybe the runner at second hit a double and the pitcher walked the next hitter to place runners on first and second. Possibly the pitcher walked both hitters, or there was a runner on first, a ground ball to an infielder was booted, and now instead of a double play and no one on, there are runners at first and second base.

It's understandable that the pitcher is at least flustered by the runners on first and second and is not paying much attention to the base runners. Remember, it is the primary responsibility of the pitcher to get the next hitter out. Pitchers are taught to regard the hitter as their primary focus. The infielders' role is to hold the runners close to keep them from stealing the next base. However, few infielders seem to know how to force a runner back if he does have a good lead or at least keep him flat-footed so it is more difficult to steal.

The defense wants to hold the runners close, but there is usually little effort to do so early in the count. The effort to hold runners on usually comes after the defense sees a threat to steal. By this time, if the runners are serious about pulling off a double steal, they should already be in motion early in the count.

Base runners in a first-and-second double-steal situation can't know how many pitches will be made to the next hitter. Each pitch could mean the runners are moving on contact, a play that eliminates the double steal. If there are no outs, a coach may decide to bunt on the first or second pitch to move the runners up. My preference is to steal the bases and save the out. The earlier in the count, the better the opportunity to make it happen successfully.

Pitchers have become rote through the years, sadly leaving athleticism behind to a large degree. As a group, they have lost their ability to move around the mound with rhythm and ease. Because pitchers don't vary their looks much today, it's that much easier for base runners to steal.

Add to this the fact that a majority of pickoff signals, even in the major leagues, come from the bench. Coaches are rarely prepared to call those pickoffs on the first pitch because their focus also is on the hitter. Just like the pitcher, coaches often don't focus on the base runners. This too adds to the base runner's advantage.

In almost all amateur leagues, even down to those with kids 8 to 10 years of age, pitches are called from the bench. Usually the same coach calls the pitches and pickoffs. This saves the catcher from having to look into the dugout for multiple coaches. The problem is that the coach has to switch back and forth from a pitch-calling to a defensive mode. This is difficult to do well and still keep the pitcher in some kind of rhythm. Once again, the hitter receives most of the attention.

If a catcher is a true gamer and understands the instinctive details of the game well, a coach should not have to call any signals during a game. A coach and catcher should discuss strategy and signals in the dugout between innings. The coach can continue to teach but not while a hitter is at the plate. A catcher matures quickly when assuming pitch-calling responsibilities.

Some pitchers, with or without a signal from the bench, use an inside move to force the base runner to hesitate. For an inside move, from the stretch position the pitcher lifts his front leg and spins the leg back toward second base. This move is not very productive for the pitcher but is used to try to deceive the runner. The key is for runners to realize that rarely is a middle infielder at the base to catch the throw when the pitcher makes his turn. It seems almost all of the inside moves today are for show only and not actual pick-off attempts. This makes it simple for the base runner to honor the move. However, it does not deter the base runner from stealing if he has the rhythm of base stealing down.

A base runner is at his most confident and aggressive after he first reaches base because no one has had the chance to make him hesitate. This makes it ideal to attempt the double steal on the first pitch or at least very early in the count. Base runners know the infielders, pitcher, and coaches are rarely prepared to give them much attention prior to the first pitch to the next batter. So if the base runners are prepared to move on the first pitch, they are more relaxed than at any time during a count. If for any reason the lead runner does not get an excellent jump on the first pitch and shuts it down, the runners still have the opportunity to run early in the count. They have more than one pitch or chance to steal before much defensive pressure is applied.

Anticipation

Both runners should be mentally and physically in sync when preparing for a double steal. Each runner knows he must make his move ahead of the pitcher. With a runner on second base, some pitchers look once and others consistently look twice. Pitchers who do a decent job of holding runners on vary their looks. When the runners anticipate together, their physical movements are usually more in sync, so the runner at first base is rarely left flat-footed as the runner on second gets a good jump and slides into third base safely.

Stealing From Second

The runner on second base has multiple options on how to approach a double steal. Some runners like to take a standing lead, although I do not advocate this kind of lead. These runners need about a 25- to 28-foot (7.6-8.5 m) standing lead and above-average speed to safely execute the steal.

The trail runner should watch the lead runner once the ball is delivered to home plate. The runner on first base usually has an easy read with a standing-lead base stealer ahead of him because such a runner takes off with little or no movement before the pitcher moves. However, the trail runner should always be aware that the lead runner can put on the brakes at any time, so the trail runner needs to keep his head up and eyes on the lead runner.

Some runners take a walking lead at second base. These base stealers usually walk a little and then stop or stutter step as they progress to a larger lead and then continue to walk. They rarely use decoy movements because they are working to take the walk into a sprint without any hesitation.

The trail runner needs to watch the lead runner once the ball is delivered to home plate. The runner on first base hesitates slightly due to the lead runner's pattern: walking, stopping, walking, and then ideally sprinting toward a steal. Again, the trail runner should always be aware that the lead runner can put on the brakes at any time.

Lead runners using the jump lead are the most difficult for the trail runner to read because of the lead's many components. The lead runner may lean with the left shoulder or take a short jab step back toward second base to load the left leg as a decoy against the defense. As the base stealer explodes off the left leg toward third base, he may or may not be running. The lead runner must try to perfectly time his movement with the pitcher's head turn back toward home plate and leg lift. Without this timing, the runner should shut down the steal even if he has taken several steps toward third base.

The lead runner turning the jump lead into a sprint may incorporate more than one jump before deciding to steal if the pitcher looks back more than once to second base. This makes it very difficult not only on the defense but also on the trail runner to read when the lead runner is actually going to take off to third base.

In this situation, the trail runner should use small jump leads almost in sync with the lead runner. This keeps the trail runner's mind and body alive and prepared to explode into a sprint just behind the lead runner's sprint. When the trail runner is jumping with the lead runner, his head is up and his eyes are taking in the lead runner's actions. The trail runner's head should stay up and focused on the lead runner until the trail runner is absolutely sure the lead runner is in a sprint to third base and is not going to stop down the line, which would place the trail runner in jeopardy of being picked off.

Trail Runner Options

The trail runner should never feel like he has to steal when the lead runner does. The preference is certainly to run at the same time. However, if the trail runner does not have a good jump, he should stay at first base. The worst-case scenario is a trail runner out of sync with the lead runner, unable to get a good jump, and thrown out at second base.

Catchers know very early in the first-and-second double-steal play whether they can possibly throw the runner out at third base. When a catcher doubts he can make the out at third, he immediately tries to throw the runner out at second base, knowing that often the trail runner is not in sync with the lead runner. This gives the catcher a small window of opportunity to throw out the trail runner.

The trail runner should feel comfortable with his lead in a potential first-and-second double-steal situation and not worry about the catcher picking him off. This is especially true if a left-handed hitter is at the plate, but even with a right-handed hitter, the runner should still be aggressive. When the double steal is on, the catcher's first option is to throw to third base, his second option is to second base, and if the base stealers are out of sync, the catcher might throw to first base, although this is rare. If the trail runner falls out of rhythm with the lead runner, he should stay at first base. This sets up a potential first-and-third double steal.

FIRST-AND-THIRD DOUBLE STEAL AGAINST A RIGHT-HANDED PITCHER

The first-and-third double steal (see figure 10.2) is another exciting play when executed well by the base stealers. The runners must practice regularly to be in sync, whether against a right- or left-handed pitcher.

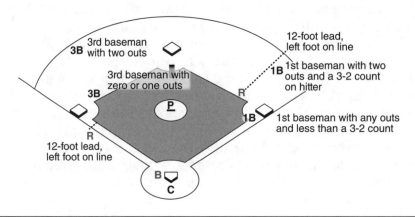

Figure 10.2 First-and-third double steal against a right-handed pitcher.

Runner at First

With a teammate at third base and a right-handed pitcher on the mound, the runner at first base has many options when initiating a potential double steal. Before the runner at first starts the front end of a potential double steal, he anticipates the pitcher's and defense's movement. The runner has a host of steals at his disposal to keep the pitcher and defense off guard. He can fake a steal, use a controlled jump lead steal, try a leaning lead steal, execute a straight steal, or attempt a delayed steal, along with many other techniques designed to place pressure on the defense. Each of these steals gives the defense a different look and may give the runner at third base a better opportunity to score.

With a runner at third base, the runner moving from first on any kind of steal except a straight steal should look back as if carrying out the hit-and-run to see if the catcher is throwing to second base, holding the ball, or throwing to third base. Once the runner on first reads the catcher's reaction, he turns his head back toward the grass in front of second base to see if one of the middle infielders moved to possibly cut off the ball short of second base. If the second baseman or shortstop has moved into this area, the infielder will cut off the ball almost 100 percent of the time. The runner does not want to stop short of the base and get in a rundown when the ball did not go to the base so he should continue straight into the base after reading that the infielder is in the grass. If the runner doesn't see an infielder in the infield grass in front of second base and the catcher is throwing toward second base, the runner should stop and try to get into a rundown. This gives the runner at third base a good opportunity to score.

Hit-and-Run Steal

A few coaches like to use the hit-and-run steal with runners at first and third. The runner at first delays just a fraction to make sure the pitcher does not fake the throw to third and then throw to first to pick off the base runner. Once the base stealer at first reads that the pitcher is definitely throwing home, he takes off. After three or four steps, the runner looks back to see if the hitter has made contact with the ball, since the hitter is supposed to protect the runner. If the hitter did not make contact, and there are no outs or one out, the runner should continue all the way to second base for an attempted straight steal. Since the runner delayed a little, he has a lower chance of being safe. However, the catcher has to respect the runner at third base and may also be delayed a split second by glancing to see if the runner at third is breaking for home.

When the hitter makes contact, the runner at first should pick up the flight of the baseball. If the runner does not find the baseball off the bat, he should look at the third-base coach for direction on whether to stop and return to first base or continue running. The coach should place his arms above his head and point skyward to tell the runner to stop and return to the base or let his arms hang down to indicate the ball is on the ground and the runner should continue to move toward the next base.

Straight Steal

If the runner at first uses a straight steal with no outs or one out, he should delay a fraction of a second to make sure the pitcher is definitely throwing home and not using the fake to third and throw to first. After that he should attempt the steal without looking back. The runner's actions are not dependent on the runner at third base since this is a straight steal.

With two outs, the runner should look back to see what the catcher does. He may decide to hold the ball, throw to third base, or throw a line drive to the pitcher or an infielder who has come in short of second base. In each of these defensive plays, the base runner reads the throw, and since the catcher is not trying to throw him out at second base, the runner continues the steal into second safely.

Delayed Steal

The delayed steal can be used with runners at first and third with no outs or one out, although it works best with two outs. In a delayed steal, the runner has much more difficulty knowing he will steal the base safely if the catcher reacts properly. The runner waits until the pitcher throws the ball toward home plate and takes his secondary shuffle lead as the ball leaves the pitcher's hand. He takes off to second base as the ball crosses the plate and looks back to see if the catcher is throwing to second. If the shortstop or second baseman is at the bag and the throw will definitely beat the runner, the runner should stop and put the defense in a rundown. This helps the runner at third base to possibly steal home. However, if either the shortstop or second baseman is in the infield grass in front of second base, the runner should continue into the base as if it were a straight steal because rarely does an infielder in the infield grass allow the ball to carry to the base.

Early Steal

The runner on first can also use the early steal. The runner begins to steal second while the pitcher is holding the ball to see if the pitcher reacts maturely or panics and possibly balks. This steal is best used with two outs and is explained further in the next section.

Runner at Third

With a right-handed pitcher on the mound and the runner at first base stealing, the runner at third employs a number of leads and reads before deciding whether to try to steal home. The minimum lead is four steps, with the left foot landing on an imaginary line approximately 12 feet (3.7 m) from the base. This is the same distance practiced at first base for a primary lead, although at first the defender holds the runner on the base. Normally the third baseman is away from the base a minimum of 12 feet except late in the game when the corner infield defenders may be playing the line.

When the pitcher picks up his leg, the base runner should begin his controlled steps toward home plate but realize that the right-handed pitcher can step directly to third base with a throw. The runner has a balanced lead when moving toward home plate so he can return to third base safely if the pitcher decides to try a pickoff.

If the pitcher releases the ball toward home plate, the runner should watch the baseball as it leaves the pitcher's hand and turn his eyes immediately to the plate while continuing to take small controlled steps down the line. Most runners cover 24 to 26 feet (7.3-7.9 m) with a walking lead outside the baseline by the time the catcher receives the ball with a right-handed hitter at the plate.

The runner should focus on the lower half of the catcher's body instead of the general area of home plate, a focus also helpful for a runner involved in a squeeze play. This way the runner picks up whether the catcher is going to fall to his knees for a quick pickoff throw to third base or step up for a pitchout, which allows the catcher to cheat early and possibly make a quicker and better throw to second or third base. This focus on the catcher's lower half is even more important with a left-handed hitter at the plate since the catcher has a wide-open shot to make a throw to third base.

After the runner at third reads the catcher's movement behind the plate and the catcher receives the ball, the runner reads the ball out of the catcher's hand. Many runners guess what the catcher will do and put themselves in a defensive running mode. If the runner reads the ball out of the catcher's hand, he is much more likely to make a good decision.

The catcher can throw the ball through to second base, throw to third base, fake a throw, or casually hold the baseball. Sometimes the catcher makes a line-drive throw toward second so the pitcher can catch it and immediately look to third to make a throw. The most difficult read for the runner is the throw through to second base.

Catchers normally throw toward second base in one of two ways. The line-drive throw travels flat and low over the mound and can be cut off by the pitcher or travel through toward second base. This throw makes it difficult for the runner at third base to leave immediately after the baseball leaves the catcher's hand so the runner must hesitate. This hesitation is good but many times prevents the runner from being able to steal home if the throw continues through to second base.

The arcing throw heads slightly upward as the ball leaves the catcher's hand. This throw has less velocity and is more difficult for the pitcher to cut off, making it easier for the runner at third base to continue moving toward the plate instead of hesitating a split second. If he times it correctly, the base runner has a much better chance to be safe at home when he reads this throw out of the catcher's hand.

The runner at third should always read the first-base runner's reaction to the catcher's throw if it goes toward second base. If the runner moving from first to second base were to stop, no matter the outs, and get caught in a rundown, the runner at third base could possibly steal home. This could also help the runner in the rundown avoid a tag by moving the defense's attention and a potential throw to either third base or home plate.

The runner at third base may fake a steal attempt home during the rundown, which helps increase his lead off third base. As the ball is being thrown back and forth between first and second base, the runner at third should look for the best possible moment to make the sprint to home plate, ideally during a longer throw from first toward second. If the runner breaks during this throw, the fielder catching the baseball has the longest throw to home plate because he is in the middle of the infield.

FIRST-AND-THIRD DOUBLE STEAL AGAINST A LEFT-HANDED PITCHER

Base runners on first and third apply the same fundamentals against a left-handed pitcher (see figure 10.3) as they do against a right-hander. *Anticipation* of the pitcher's movements is key. The runner on third base needs to remember that the pitcher doesn't have as clear a view of him as he does the runner on first and should try to take advantage of this.

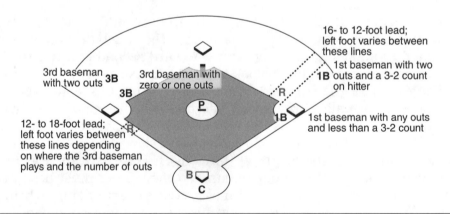

Figure 10.3 First-and-third double steal against a left-handed pitcher.

Runner at First

With a left-handed pitcher on the mound, the base runner should first anticipate a pitcher's movements. The concentration is primarily on the pitcher's lead leg and reading whether the pitcher uses it to try to deceive the runner with a throw to first or home. However, some left-handed pitchers step off with the back foot and make a snap throw to first base, so the runner must be aware of this potential pickoff move as well.

The base runner at first may try a straight steal from a standing lead, use a leaning lead, use a short lead with a controlled jump, or run on the first movement of the pitcher's right side. The runner may also use a delayed steal or leave early while the pitcher is still holding the ball. Each of these steals gives the defense a different look and may give the runner at third base a better opportunity to score.

A trick play a runner can use against a left-handed pitcher is to take a very large lead to try to draw a throw, since the left-handed pitcher can see the runner is extremely far off the base. As the pitcher throws to first, the runner falls down on his right side about 15 to 20 feet (4.6-6 m) off the base. The runner is hoping the first baseman will panic and run out to tag him. While the first baseman is concentrating on the fallen runner, the runner on third sprints toward home hoping the first baseman's slight distraction gives the runner just enough time to score.

With a runner at third base, the runner moving from first base on any kind of steal except a straight steal looks back as if running on a hit and run to see if the catcher throws to second base, holds the ball, or throws to third base.

Once the runner from first reads the catcher, he turns his head back toward second base and looks into the grass area in front of second base to see if one of the middle infielders is there to possibly cut off the ball short of second base. If the second baseman or shortstop moved into this area, the infielder will cut off the ball almost 100 percent of the time. The runner does not want to stop short of the base to get into a rundown if the ball does not go to the base. The runner should continue straight into the base after reading the infielder in the grass.

If the runner looks into the grass portion of the infield in front of the second base bag and doesn't see an infielder and the catcher throws through toward second base, the runner should stop and try to get into a rundown. This will give the runner at third base a good opportunity score before the third out is recorded.

Hit-and-Run Steal

Some coaches like to use the hit and run with runners at first and third. With a left-handed pitcher on the mound, the runner should delay slightly to make sure the throw goes home. The base stealer at first reads the pitcher's throws home and takes off. On a hit and run, the hitter is supposed to protect the runner by swinging the bat, so after three or four steps the runner looks back to see if the hitter made contact. If the hitter did not make contact, and there are no or one outs, the runner continues all the way to second base in an attempted straight steal. Because of the delay, there is a lower percentage chance the runner will be safe. However the catcher has to watch the runner at third base, which will give the runner from first a slight advantage. The catcher may also delay a split second to see if the runner at third will break for home.

When the hitter makes contact, the runner picks up the flight of the baseball. If the runner does not find the ball off the bat, he should look to the third-base coach for direction on whether to stop and return to first base or continue to second. The coach places his arms above his head and points to the sky to tell the runner to stop and return to the base or he lets his arms hang down to indicate the ball is on the ground and the runner should continue to move into second base.

Straight Steal

If the runner at first uses a straight steal with no outs or one out, he must still delay a little with a left-handed pitcher on the mound unless he is running on first movement. However, coaches rarely use first-movement steals with runners at first and third base. The defense is in a tough situation, so the offense should use a higher-percentage steal than first movement. When using a straight steal, the runner should try not to look back. The runner's actions are not dependent on the runner at third base since this is a straight steal. With two outs, the runner should look back to read the catcher's reaction and see if he makes a throw.

Delayed Steal

Although it's best to use the delayed steal with two outs, it can be used with runners at first and third with no or one outs. The technique for the delayed steal is the same against a right-handed or left-handed pitcher. During a delayed steal, the runner has a more difficult time knowing definitively he can steal the base safely if the catcher reacts properly. For the delayed steal, the runner takes his secondary shuttle lead as the ball leaves the pitcher's hand toward home plate. The runner takes off to second base as the ball crosses the plate. The runner looks back to see if the catcher is throwing to second base. If the shortstop or second baseman is at the bag and the throw will definitely beat the runner, the runner stops and tries to get the defense into a rundown. This gives the runner at third time to attempt to steal home. If either middle infielder is in the infield grass in front of second base, the runner should continue to the base as if it was a straight steal. Rarely will an infielder in the grass allow the ball to carry to the base.

Runner at First Leaves Early

This steal can catch a left-handed pitcher by surprise since he is looking directly at the runner and not expecting him to take off. This steal is best used with two outs.

Runner on First is Running With Two Outs

The stealing options available to the runner on first are the same with two outs as with less than two outs. The runner may leave on the pitcher's movement or from a standing still lead, a leaning lead, or a controlled jump lead. He may use a delayed steal or leave early while the pitcher is holding the ball to try to draw a balk.

With two outs, the runner should always look back to pick up the catcher's action. If the catcher is throwing toward second base and the runner knows he is going to beat the throw, he continues directly into the base. He also continues toward second if he sees the catcher will not make a throw at all. If the runner sees the catcher is throwing to second base and the runner feels he will be out at second, he must stop short of the base and get into a rundown to give the runner at third a good chance to steal home before the third out is made.

After the runner from first base looks back to the plate for the catcher's reaction, his head turns toward the middle of the infield. If the runner sees a middle infielder in the grass in front of second base, he continues into the base. Rarely will an infielder in this position allow the ball to travel to the base. The infielder is in the grass to cut off the ball and catch the runner at third moving toward home plate.

Runner at Third

With a left-handed pitcher on the mound and the runner at first base stealing, the runner at third employs a number of leads and reads before deciding whether to try to steal home. The minimum lead brings the runner's left foot to an imaginary line 15 to 18 feet (4.6-5.5 m) from the bag. Because the left-handed pitcher has his back to the runner, the runner can take a larger lead than against a right-hander. Normally the third baseman is away from the base a minimum of 12 feet except late in the game when the corner infield defenders may be playing the line.

When the pitcher raises his leg, the base runner takes controlled steps toward home plate, realizing the pitcher may still throw to first base. If the pitcher throws to first, the runner maintains his walk down the third-base line until he is forced to stop. The runner is balanced in his lead. He begins the move toward home plate so he can return to the base safely if the first baseman throws across the infield after the pickoff at first base.

If the pitcher releases the ball toward home, the runner watches the ball as it leaves the pitcher's hand then immediately turns his eyes to the plate, continuing to take small, controlled steps down the line. Most runners will reach 24 to 26 feet (7.3-7.9 m) after completing the walking lead outside the baseline when the catcher receives the ball with a right-handed hitter at the plate. With a left-handed hitter at the plate, the lead can be the same distance but the base runner must be more aware that the catcher has an open lane to make a pickoff throw to third base.

The runner looks at the lower half of the catcher's body. All base runners should learn this fundamental for stealing from third base. This also is the correct place for the runner to focus if he were involved in a squeeze or safety squeeze play.

By focusing on the lower half of the catcher's body instead of the general area of home plate, the runner will be able to determine if the catcher is going to fall to his knees for a quick pickoff throw to third or step up for a pitchout, which allows the catcher to cheat early and hopefully make a quicker, better throw to second or third. This focus on the catcher's lower half is even more important with a left-handed hitter at the plate since the catcher has a wide open shot to make a throw to third.

After observing the catcher's body movements behind the plate and seeing the catcher catch the ball, the runner reads the ball out of the catcher's hand. Many runners guess what the catcher will do; this places the runner in a defensive baserunning mode. If the runner reads the ball out of the catcher's hand, the runner is more likely to make a good decision.

The catcher's options are to throw through to second, throw to third, fake a throw, or casually hold the baseball. Sometimes the catcher will throw a line drive, low-trajectory ball toward second, and the pitcher will catch the ball and immediately look to make a throw to third.

The most difficult read for the runner is the throw through to second base. Catchers use two types of throws to go to second base, the flat trajectory throw and the arcing throw.

The flat trajectory throw is a line drive that travels low over the mound and can be cut off by the pitcher or travel through to second. On this type of throw, the runner at third will not be able to leave immediately after the ball leaves the catcher's hand. He must hesitate in case the pitcher cuts off the throw. This is why a runner must read the play instead of trying to guess what will happen after the throw is delivered. This hesitation is good, but may prevent the runner from safely stealing home if the throw continues through to second base.

The arcing throw heads up slightly as the ball leaves the catcher's hand. This throw has less velocity and is more difficult for the pitcher to cut off, making it easier for the runner at third to continue moving toward the plate without hesitating. If he times it correctly, the base runner has a better chance to be safe at home after reading this throw out of the catcher's hand.

The catcher may fake or hold the ball. In this case, the runner must stay balanced and not be tricked into leaning too much or straying too far off base.

The runner on third should not predetermine he will break for home plate if the ball is thrown through to second base. Multiple situations can occur with runners at first and third, and the runner must consider all factors including the score, inning, and number of outs.

Most coaches will allow the runner to make the decision. The runner should anticipate a throw through to second base so his mind and body work together ahead of his sprint toward the plate. But the runner should physically react after reading the baseball so he makes the right decision.

PRESET STEAL OF HOME

Preset plays are designed and practiced to work on base stealing or just trying to draw a throw from a pitcher or catcher, but they are difficult to execute in a game no matter how often or how efficiently they have been practiced. These plays usually involve two runners on base but can also work with the bases loaded. Coaches should prepare as well as possible for the unexpected when running a preset play. One of the most popular preset running plays is the double steal at first and third base with a left-handed pitcher (see figure 10.4).

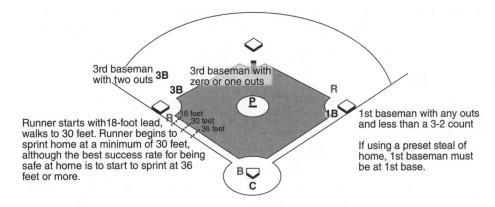

Figure 10.4 Preset double steal with runners on first and third against a left-handed pitcher.

The runner at first base wants the left-handed pitcher to try to pick him off. The runner at third base knows the runner at first is trying to draw a throw, so the runner at third sets up his lead and anticipates the throw so he can react toward the plate. The runner at first base has many ways to draw a throw off a left-handed pitcher since the pitcher is looking directly at him. The runner can take an extra-large lead to get the pitcher's attention and encourage him to throw over. The runner can take a normal lead and begin to lean toward second base on the right leg as if he has lost his balance. Some runners actually fall onto their right sides to draw the throw; if the pitcher throws, they bounce up immediately and head toward second base. The runner can begin his steal on the first movement of the pitcher's right side and hope the pitcher still throws behind the runner to first base.

If the runner draws a throw, no matter the outs, he wants to continue to draw the attention of the first baseman so the runner at third can begin to sprint home without a lot of attention. The runner wants to make sure he is not tagged out immediately by the first baseman but makes him apply the tag by running all the way to second base or throwing the ball past the runner to a middle infielder so the runner can stop and get into a rundown.

The runner at third should be able to take an extra-large 18- to 21-foot (5.5-6.4 m) initial lead without attracting the pitcher's attention since the pitcher has his back to the runner. An even larger lead might be possible with many left-handed hitters at the plate today since teams sometimes play an overshift.

Once the pitcher moves into the stretch position, the runner at third anticipates him lifting his right leg. *Anticipation* is critical in helping the runner start on time to make this steal attempt a reality. The runner stands about 20 feet (6 m) off third base before the pitcher sets. As the pitcher's arms head to the set position, the base runner takes an additional two to four steps, which means the runner is as far as 30 to 32 feet (9.1-9.8 m) off the bag when the pitcher lifts his leg to either throw to first base or home. This distance helps ensure that the runner has a chance to score if he continues to react properly on this play.

When the pitcher lifts the right leg, the base runner at third should immediately start a controlled sprint toward home plate. This could place the runner as far down the line as 45 feet (13.7 m), which is halfway to home plate. The runner keeps his head toward the pitcher until the pitcher has committed to throw to first base or home plate.

If the pitcher makes the throw to first instead of home plate, the runner's controlled sprint at about 45 feet turns into a full sprint to home plate with the anticipation of a feet-first slide to the third-base side of the plate due to a possible throw from the first baseman. There can be no hesitation once the pitcher throws to first since the base runner is already halfway home.

However, if the left-handed pitcher turns the right leg toward the plate to throw, the runner must apply the brakes and sprint back toward third base with no hesitation to anticipate a throw from the catcher if the batter takes the pitch. The runner on third does not have the luxury of hanging out down the baseline in this situation. The runner's back could be to home plate if the hitter makes contact, but that is the chance taken with this attempted preset steal of home.

The runner at first either stays at first base or has committed to second before the pickoff throw from the pitcher. If he's moving, he decides whether to use a decoy movement, leave on the pitcher's first movement, or head toward second on a straight steal. He anticipates the defense's response, especially with two outs. A base runner who begins the steal with less than two outs should continue all the way to second base and try to draw a throw and allow the runner at third to score. With two outs, the runner should try to draw a throw and get in a rundown to again give the runner at third base a better opportunity to score.

Live Defense Versus Live Base Runners

OBJECTIVES

Learn various decoys, jumps, and steals. Learn to read the flight of the ball out of the catcher's hand. Learn to read the movements of left- and right-handed pitchers. Learn to read the movements of the middle infielders on plays at second base.

EQUIPMENT

Full infield area, baseballs and bases.

EXECUTION

Runners at first, second, and third and the infield defense get in position. The pitchers throw to home plate and first, second, and third base. Catchers throw to all bases and in some situations go directly back to the pitcher, fake the throw, or hold the ball. The runners at first and second base work in sync to pull off the straight double steal with the runner at second using the standing, walking, and jump leads. When runners work on the first-and-third double steal, the runner at first uses the straight steal, delayed steal, fake steal, jump lead steal off a right- or left-handed pitcher or a first-movement steal off a left-handed pitcher. The runner at first base practices getting caught in a rundown between the bases, and the runner at third reads the defense to learn when to break for home plate.

(continued)

(continued)

COACHING POINTS

Base stealers learn to read pitchers and throws. Pitchers learn to hold runners. The defense learns to handle the baseball as runners try to steal.

Part Four

Strength and Conditioning

Today's baseball players work hard to maintain their power, speed, agility, and endurance in an effort to stay ahead of the defense. Developing a powerful body takes hard work and commitment. Base runners use multiplanar movements because they work the body in more than one plane of movement, mimicking the actions of the runner on the basepath. Powerful legs are important but not the whole picture. A complete base runner also needs a strong core to help maintain proper running form and a fit upper body to help him explosively move from base to base.

For the base runner, speed and quickness are two sides of the same coin. A complete base runner develops both to help him outwit pitchers and infielders and keep the defense alert. Ladder, sprinting, and bounding drills help the runner perfect his form and increase his stride frequency.

Knowing what to do is part of the art of conditioning; knowing the best time to do it is as well. Proper timing of conditioning helps the baseball player peak at just the right time to take him through a long season and beyond. A well-designed off-season training plan ensures that the player is physically prepared for all aspects of the game.

Developing Power

The word *power* is used quite often in baseball and refers to both pitchers and hitters. Power is needed for most sports, but some sports are specifically considered power sports. Football, basketball, hockey, and volleyball are examples because they use short, explosive movements and do not require long, sustained activity. Baseball is no exception and may be one of the best examples of a power sport.

POWER VERSUS STRENGTH

Many coaches and players often confuse strength with power. While strength and power go together, they are not the same and need to be developed and trained for separately.

In the world of performance training, strength is the ability to generate as much force as possible during one repetition of an exercise. This is known as 1 repetition maximum, or 1RM. As an equation, the formula for strength looks like this: strength = mass × distance. In other words, it refers to moving an object (mass) a certain length (distance). Notice that there is no concept of time in this equation. When it comes to resistance training, good examples of pure strength exercises are the maximum squat and maximum bench press. It doesn't matter how long it takes to complete these tasks, only that they are completed. Moving these heavy loads slowly does not matter, even in competition, as long as the lift, or movement, is completed.

Power, on the other hand, involves speed of movement, and the time it takes to complete the task is very important. Power as an equation looks like this: power = work ÷ time. Power often is referred to as speed–strength. Good examples of performance power movements are the power clean and vertical jump.

POWER IN BASEBALL

Imagine trying to hit a baseball without speed. A hitter may be very strong but still not possess speed. This is where power comes in; without power there is no speed. *Bat speed* is the term used in baseball. Without power, the strongest baseball hitter in the world would not hit the ball out of the infield.

If a pitcher has a power arm, he has very good arm speed. Without power, the strongest pitcher would not get the ball to the plate. Baserunning and defense also require power and what is called first-step quickness, the ability to get a good jump on a ball in the field or toward the next base when stealing or trying to score.

BUILDING POWER

Most traditional weight-lifting programs work on developing strength, but power development is also key when designing a baseball-specific training program. Baserunning and base stealing improve with increased lower-body power.

Several strategies work to develop power. First, increasing the speed of a lift return works on power development. Take the squat for instance. A good rule of thumb for the beginner is to lower the weight in a slow and controlled manner (about 2 seconds), pause slightly (about 1 second) at the bottom, and then return to the starting position in about the same time as it took to lower the weight (about 2 seconds). For increased power production, the tempo should be much faster. The lowering phase can still remain slower and controlled (about 2 seconds), but as soon as the weight is at the bottom of the lift, it is returned as quickly as possible without any hold.

In addition to increasing the tempo with traditional lifts, another strategy for increasing power is through the use of plyometric exercises. Plyometric exercises are movements that train muscles to reach maximum strength in the shortest possible time. These types of exercises include jumping in place, bounding, and box hops. Upper-body plyometric exercises include the medicine ball chest put or rotational toss. In general, plyometric exercises are used by athletes looking to increase their first-step quickness, vertical jump, and overall power. Plyometric exercises along with eccentric strength development through closed kinetic-chain exercises are critical for preventing injury as well as increasing power. Inappropriate application of plyometric exercises is possible if not monitored correctly. Part of proper practice when using plyometrics is to simply measure performance and have a plan.

The recommended volume of specific jumps in any one session varies with intensity and progression goals. Table 11.1 shows work volume variations for beginning, intermediate, and advanced workouts. A beginner in a single off-season session could complete 60 to 100 foot contacts of low-intensity exercise. The intermediate exerciser might be able to do 100 to 150 foot contacts of both low- and moderate-intensity exercise in one session.

Table 11.1 Plyometric Work Volume for a Baseball Player: Total Foot Strikes

	Beginner	**Intermediate**	**Advanced**	**Intensity**
Off-season	60–100	100–150	120–200	Low to moderate
Preseason	100–250	150–300	150–450	Moderate to high
In-season	50–75	75–100	100–150	High

POWERFUL LEGS FOR BASERUNNING

Most traditional leg-strengthening programs are broken down into working the quads, hamstrings, and calves. Some programs include the glutes as well. This muscle group training approach only scratches the surface of true strength development, especially when it comes to the legs. Exercises such as leg curls, leg extensions, and calf raises work with movements at only one joint and in one plane and are known as uniplanar joint movements. These exercises are great for aesthetics and certain phases of rehabilitation programs. The problem with these exercises is that there is really no functionality to them. In other words, they do not mirror the more complex movements of real life, especially in activities such as baserunning. Movement in one plane does very little to stimulate motor memory and limits the ability to move in multiple planes effectively, critical to baserunning. A good base runner must be able to react quickly and change direction on demand.

Before looking at specific multiplanar exercises, consider the planes the human body moves in. The sagittal plane divides the body into left and right halves and features movement forward, backward, up, and down. An example of a lower-body exercise in the sagittal plane is the leg extension.

The frontal plane divides the body into front and back halves and features side-to-side motions. Lower-body abduction (movement away from the midline) and adduction (movement toward the midline) movements can be performed with free weights or machines and are examples of frontal-plane movements.

The transverse plane divides the body into top and bottom halves and features mostly rotational movement. The transverse lunge (lunging with rotation) is a good example of an exercise in the transverse plane. Lower-body strength is the foundation for total-body strength. The legs and torso are connected by the hips. To build strong and powerful hips an athlete must use closed-chain multiplanar exercises.

The vast range of motion at the hip joint (flexion, extension, abduction, adduction, internal rotation, and external rotation) makes multiplanar exercises a must in a well-rounded program. Multiplanar movements develop strong, functional legs; help build quickness and agility for baseball; and increase stability and ease of movement for everyday activities.

POWERFUL CORE

Core strength and power are a big part of success in baseball. The area of the body below the chest and above the thighs is critical for transferring strength and power from the lower to upper body. Proper throwing, sprinting, and hitting mechanics suffer without a strong core. Base runners benefit from a strong and powerful core as well. Baserunning may suffer if the player is not able to hold proper sprint mechanics due to a weak core. A strong and stable core may also assist in injury prevention when sliding and diving head first. The ballistic rotational demands of hitting and throwing can be very hard on the torso and lower back. A strong core helps to increase performance and decrease the chances of injury.

DEVELOPING A POWERFUL UPPER BODY

Most athletes and coaches think only of the lower body when it comes to power, but the upper body can be trained for power too. The use of medicine balls and resistive cables allows the strength and conditioning coach to create explosive upper-body movement. Plyometric push-ups, medicine ball chest puts, and cable punches and pulls are examples of explosive exercises designed to develop power in the upper body. A powerful upper body is a must for hitting and throwing. Base runners benefit from a powerful arm swing across the body when advancing to the next base after a lead as well as a powerful arm swing forward to back when accelerating to top speed.

Speed and Quickness

Speed and quickness are important components of most sports, and baseball is no exception. Speed is one of five tools that college and professional scouts measure when looking at a player (the others are hitting for average, hitting for power, arm strength, and fielding). Increasing speed and quickness, like any other area of player development, takes tremendous work and consistency.

In baseball, speed, or the time it takes to get from point A to point B, usually is measured with the 60-yard dash, a test that has been used by scouts for decades to measure straight-ahead speed. Quickness, or the ability to get to top speed as fast as possible, is more difficult to measure and may also include reaction time and change of direction. Most scouts consider quickness more along the lines of hard-to-measure qualities like instinct or baseball awareness.

Every baseball player with the proper training should be able to make gains in speed and quickness, regardless of his starting point. Improving sprint speed and foot quickness means understanding the two components of sprinting: stride length and stride frequency. Stride length is simply the distance covered during the sprint cycle and is best improved through gains in strength and flexibility. Stride frequency is the number of cycles covered in a given distance. Stride frequency gains are best made by improvements in specific neuromuscular pathway recruitments, or teaching the nerves to fire the muscles in a coordinated manner that allows for efficient movement. Stride length and stride frequency combined make up an athlete's overall speed. Sprinting mechanics, just like pitching or hitting mechanics, must be developed and worked on regularly. A baseball player who wants to get faster must work on all aspects of speed development.

IMPROVING STRIDE LENGTH

Stride length is best improved by increasing strength, mostly in the lower body, and range of motion, especially in the hips and lower body, but increased strength in the core and even upper body is also very important for developing speed. Exercises such as squats, lunges, and step-ups increase overall lower-body strength. These exercises are multijoint movements; that is, they require flexion and extension at the ankles, knees, and hips. Sprinting requires strong, powerful movements at these three joints.

While strength is important for increasing stride length, the other part of the equation is range of motion at and around these same joints. An optimal stride length (somewhere in the range of 1.14 to 1.35 times the athlete's height) is a byproduct of strength and flexibility. Dynamic range-of-motion exercises such as walking lunges, leg swings, and lateral lunges assist in developing a fluid stride.

INCREASING STRIDE FREQUENCY

Increasing stride frequency is the most difficult improvement to make when trying to increase speed. An athlete can improve his stride frequency through regular sprinting drills and proper sprinting mechanics that create specific neuromuscular pathways. Examples of sprinting drills that stimulate this motor-learning process include hill running or incline sprinting on a high-speed treadmill, skips, and bounding. Proper mechanics are crucial to getting the most out of the strength, range of motion, and neurological pathways developed through training.

PERFECTING SPRINT MECHANICS

All skills require fundamentals that must be followed for optimal performance. Sprinting mechanics are no exception. When sprinting, the head should remain steady with the eyes looking straight ahead. The face and lower jaw should be relaxed and the shoulders down. The arms should be flexed at a 90-degree angle with relaxed hands. The thumb and index fingers should be lightly touching or the palms can stay open and relaxed with the fingers straight ahead. The elbows should be near the sides of the body and moving front to back. Crossing the arms in front of the body causes hip rotation, resulting in inefficient movement and decreased speed. The ball of the foot should strike the ground directly under the hip with a powerful push. The leg pushes backward until fully extended. The knee then drives up and forward to repeat the cycle.

SPEED AND AGILITY LADDER DRILLS

A speed or agility ladder is a great tool for working on sprint mechanics and overall foot quickness. The squares of the ladder (see figure 12.1) force the athlete to work on body control, as speed without body control is useless in most athletic endeavors. Baserunning is all about quickness and control. An out-of-control base runner will not take the proper angles on the basepath, will get poor, unbalanced jumps when trying to advance, and will simply run into outs. The following are just a few examples of speed and foot quickness drills executed with a ladder.

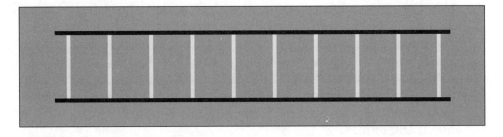

Figure 12.1 Ladder for agility and footwork drills.

Forward Speed/Agility Steps

Sprint through these exercises and walk back. Go as fast as you can once you learn the steps. Do not hit the ladder.

One foot in each square: Run through with one foot in each square.

Two feet in each square: Run through with both feet in each square.

High knees and one foot in each square: Run through the ladder with one foot in each square with your knees high and pump the arms forward and backward. Stay on the balls of your feet. Keep your trunk upright and arms at 90 degrees.

High knees and two feet in each square: Run through the ladder with two feet in each square with your knees high and pump the arms forward and backward. Stay on the balls of your feet. Keep your trunk upright and arms at 90 degrees.

Heel kicks and one foot in each square: Run through the ladder with one foot in each square while attempting to kick your buttocks with your heels. Stay on the balls of your feet and continue to swing the arms forward and backward. Keep your arms at 90 degrees.

Heel kicks and two feet in each square: Run through the ladder with two feet in each square while attempting to kick your buttocks with your heels. Stay on the balls of your feet and continue to swing the arms forward and backward, arms at 90 degrees.

Power skip: Stand tall and raise your right arm and left leg at the same time. Skip through the ladder, alternating the arm and leg sequence.

Triple step: Start with the right foot in a square. Bring the left foot into the square while taking the right foot out and to the right side of the ladder. Start back across the ladder with the left foot in the second square and then the right foot. Continue down the ladder.

Quad step: Start with the right foot in a square. Bring the left foot into the square while taking the right foot out and to the right side of the ladder. Step all the way through the ladder and touch the inside left foot to the ground. Start back into the ladder with the left foot in the second square and then bring the right foot into the second square. Take the left foot out to the left of the ladder, followed by the right foot, which now becomes the inside foot touching the ground. Repeat the sequence and continue down the ladder.

Lateral Agility Steps

Baseball involves a lot of lateral movement. Whether it is taking a lead, fielding a ground ball, or making a drop step in the outfield, baseball-specific movements are rarely straight ahead. These drills help develop quick, agile feet.

One in, one out: Stand beside the ladder. Place the right foot into the first square and the left foot into the second square and then move both feet back out. Continue the sequence down the ladder.

Two in, two out: Stand beside the ladder. Place both feet in each square and then move both feet back out. Repeat down the ladder.

One in, two out: Start with the right foot in the first square and then move both feet out. Next, move the left foot into the second square and then move both feet out. Continue the sequence down the ladder.

SPRINTING DRILLS

Sprinting up a hill is a great exercise for building leg strength and power. The incline forces the athlete to lift the knees high and strike the ground with the balls of the feet. Practice moving the arms forward to back while maintaining a 90-degree angle at the elbow. An incline of about 10 to 15 degrees should suffice for this drill.

When a hill is not available, or if the weather does not permit outdoor hill running, a high-speed treadmill may be used to accomplish the same goals. Safety is always a concern with sprinting on a treadmill, so extra caution should be taken when performing high-speed sprints. Inclines as high as 15 to 20 degrees and speeds as high as 10 to 12 miles per hour are not uncommon with this activity.

Several pieces of equipment may be added to a sprinting program to create resistance. The rationale behind resisted running is the same as with weight training: Overload the affected muscles and they will get stronger. Parachutes, sleds, resistive tubing, and even partner resistive running have all been used to add intensity to sprinting. Be aware, however, that too much resistance may lead to compromised mechanics and actually become counterproductive.

BOUNDING AND SKIPPING DRILLS

Skipping and bounding drills may be used to develop rhythm and tempo. Many variations of these drills have evolved, mostly through track and field training. The concept is to break down the sprint into smaller parts and work quickly and explosively on these areas to aid in the development of speed. Marching with an exaggerated foot strike and arm swing as well as rhythmic skipping are examples of this type of training.

Speed in baserunning and base stealing is just one component of the overall equation for success in baseball. Instincts on the basepath and learning how to read pitchers and get adequate jumps off a lead can be taught and learned, but only through consistent practice.

Off-Season Conditioning

When designing an off-season conditioning program, factor in how many days per week to train, how much resistance training is necessary, the amount of rest needed, the type of equipment available, when to work on speed development, and when and how much to throw and hit. This is known as periodization. Periodization is the process of laying out a schedule and changing up workouts to keep them effective. If a player does the same workout over and over again, his body adapts to this program and he simply does not progress any further. Setting up distinct training periods shocks the body, giving it new challenges to aid in speed, strength, and fitness gains. Manipulate the sets, reps, resistance, rest periods, and order and type of exercises to change up the routine.

TRAINING CYCLES

Typical periodized programs are divided into three basic time periods, or cycles. The first is a macrocycle, offering the "big picture" of the overall program, usually over a one-year period. Baseball players benefit from the macrocycle as they prepare for a season. The mesocycle is a medium-length time period with several phases, often performed in the 6- to 12-week range. A microcycle is a very short time period, often measured by what a player does in a given week or even day. Each macrocycle and mesocycle has multiple phases within it.

Generally a preparation phase comes first, a time during which the player prepares the body for a more intense phase to follow. This is a very general low-volume and low-intensity phase featuring speed mechanics and light fitness activities over a period of 4 to 6 weeks. This phase usually begins after a rest period enjoyed after a long baseball season.

The strength-building phase follows. This phase builds the base or foundation for the remaining phases. Building strength is key to building speed and power later on in the program. This phase usually involves moderate to high volume and moderate intensity over a period of 12 to 24 weeks. Speed work now moves beyond mechanics, and speed ladder drills and moderate-intensity sprints should be added to the program.

Next is the strength and power phase. This phase is the most intense and focuses on building pure strength and power. The strength and power phase involves moderate volume but very high intensity over a period from 4 to 8 weeks. This phase should take place just prior to the season and even into spring training for the professional player. At this point the player concentrates very hard on speed development. High-intensity sprinting such as incline treadmill running or hill training should be the focus. Resistive sprinting devices such as sleds, bands, or parachutes may also be used at this time. Toward the end of this phase, the player should consider moving toward on-field baserunning, depending on the length of the preseason.

Finally, a maintenance phase is necessary during the season to maintain gains made during the previous phases. The volume should be low but with high intensity. This phase is often misunderstood. Many old-school baseball coaches believe a maintenance phase is one of low volume and low intensity. This is simply not true. High intensity allows a player to realize strength and power gains. Speed work should continue throughout the season but on a less frequent basis, maybe once or twice a week. Most baseball seasons are several months long, and a maintenance program is a must to maintain strength and speed. The length of each phase depends on the length of the off-season and time available to train.

At the conclusion of a macrocycle a player enters a time of recovery or active rest to allow the body to heal and regenerate after a long season. This is not a time to do nothing but rather to participate in lower-intensity activities while allowing the body the time it needs to rest in preparation for the next macrocycle. This is the best time to address any minor injuries developed over the course of the season.

REPETITIONS FOR STRENGTH AND SPEED TRAINING

Over the past two decades, baseball has become a game built more around strength, speed, and power. Hitters are looking to drive the ball, pitchers are looking to power the ball past the hitters with greater velocity, and most players are looking to develop greater size.

Baseball players usually want to develop muscle strength, size, and endurance. The following repetition schemes benefit each of these areas of muscle development. The number of repetitions needed depends on a player's goals.

Muscle strength: Muscle strength is the ability to move or lift a maximum amount of weight one time (1RM). Maximum deadlifts and squats are examples of exercises that measure pure strength. The key to developing strength is to overload the muscles with very heavy weights. A good strength base is needed to develop first-step quickness and power. In order to reach this heavy overload, a player needs to keep repetitions low. Plan to perform 3 to 6 repetitions per set, a range ideal for loading the muscles to near max. Performing too many repetitions fatigues the muscles prematurely and will not be as effective in building strength. Muscles, tendons, and ligaments need to adapt to these heavy loads to improve overall strength and power.

Muscle size (hypertrophy): Muscle strength and size go hand in hand. As muscle strength increases, so does size. However, if a player mainly wants to develop size he must follow a high-volume, moderate-repetition range (8 to 12 repetitions) of moderate to high intensity. The higher work volume demanded by this scenario best promotes muscle growth. But developing size for baseball is not always a good idea. Big, bulky muscles may detract from the fluid movements required to run, throw, and swing. An athlete can favor the strength side of a hypertrophy program by doing 6 to 8 repetitions and still realize strength and size gains. High-volume (hypertrophy) training works best for young, lean players who need to increase muscle mass, but they should be sure to work through a full range of motion during lifts and maintain flexibility along the way.

Muscle endurance: Muscle endurance is the ability of muscles to perform repeated bouts of work. Swimmers, runners, and cyclists all benefit from high-repetition (15 to 20 repetitions) programs. A common misperception is that athletes in a maintenance program (especially in season) need to use lighter weights and higher repetitions to maintain strength. This is simply not true. High-repetition, low-intensity programs develop muscular endurance but are not optimal for maintaining strength gains. Muscular endurance programs are great for beginners just learning how to weight train. Using lighter weights allows a focus on proper form, whereas heavier weights can lead to poor technique and subsequent injuries.

Most baseball players really have no need for high-repetition, low-weight routines unless prescribed by a health professional for a specific purpose. Muscle endurance is important for pitchers looking to pitch later into games and those who want to accumulate a lot of innings throughout the season. Pitchers use high-repetition, low-weight routines for rotator cuff and scapular stabilizing routines.

REST

The amount of time an athlete rests between sets, training days, and cycles depends on specific training goals, season length, and the types of exercises and practices performed. For instance, longer rest periods are required when performing compound exercises as opposed to isolation movements. Complex training also requires longer rest periods between exercises. Many coaches do not consider rest periods when designing season-long baseball training programs, but overuse injuries are very common in young baseball players and most could be avoided with proper rest.

TEMPO

An exercise repetition is made up of two phases: the concentric phase, or the shortening of the muscle (often referred to as the exertion portion of the exercise); and the eccentric phase, or the lengthening of the muscle (often referred to as the negative or resisting portion of the exercise). With the squat, for example, the eccentric phase is when the hips, knees, and ankles flex and the weight is lowered. The concentric phase is when the hips, knees, and ankles extend and the weight is pushed back up to the starting position. The tempo is the rate of movement, or speed, during both the concentric and eccentric phases of the repetition.

Training tempo varies, but it is important to control the weight. A slow controlled lift is usually the safest and most effective way to perform an exercise. A rule of thumb is to lower the weight (eccentric movement) at a pace of 2 to 4 seconds and lift or push the weight at a pace of 1 to 3 seconds.

Baserunning requires the right tempo. Speed is often considered the only component needed to become a good base stealer or base runner. As a result, sometimes base runners appear out of control. For success on the basepath, proper tempo and balance should not be overlooked.

DYNAMIC WARM-UP AND FLEXIBILITY

Many baseball coaches confuse stretching with warming up and use stretching to warm up before a practice or game. There is a distinct difference between warming up and stretching. In fact, stretching may not even be necessary before a practice or game. A warm-up is much more important.

The warm-up elevates the heart rate and increases the temperature of the muscles, tendons, ligaments, and joints. A cold, static stretch routine simply can't do this. Start with a general warm-up, such as a light jog or running the bases at a very light pace. Either of these activities increases the heart rate and begins the warm-up necessary to prepare the body for the more intense exercise or practice to follow. Five minutes is probably enough time to spend on the general warm-up. Spending too much time here compromises the quality of the strength, speed, or practice session.

The general warm-up should be followed by an active or dynamic warm-up routine. Leg swings, lying hip rotations, walking lunges, and over-under hurdle walks are great ways to increase range of motion in and around the joints and muscles. This routine adds about 5 minutes to the warm-up.

The final stage of the warm-up routine should be done with weights if preparing for a strength workout, sprint mechanics if preparing for a speed workout, or light baseball skills if preparing for a baseball practice. Postworkout or postgame stretching is great for cooling down and helping to maintain flexibility. This is the time for additional static stretching to work on range of motion or decrease stiffness.

RESISTANCE TRAINING AND INJURY PREVENTION SPLIT DESIGNS

It's now time to put the program together. A training split details what the weekly schedule looks like. Individual programs should be designed based on goals and time available. An athlete first decides on how many days per week he will devote to strength training, speed training, and skill work. Plan on resistance training two or three times per week if size and strength are desired. Once an athlete determines how many days per week he will train, his next decision is for how long. There are virtually hundreds of split designs to choose from. Here are two basic routines.

Whole-body split (three times per week): The whole-body split is the simplest way to train all the muscle groups in one session. An example is to strength train on Monday, Wednesday, and Friday or Tuesday, Thursday, and Saturday, making sure to have one full day of recovery between strength-training sessions. The biggest advantage of this type of routine is that it limits gym visits to only three days per week, ideal for those with limited time. The downside is that it demands a long time in the gym on those training days due to the high volume of exercises performed. Limit rest time between sets if necessary in order to speed up the workout. Table 13.1 shows an example of a whole-body split.

Table 13.1   Whole-Body Training Split

Day	Area trained
Monday	Lower body, upper body, shoulder and elbow maintenance, core, scapula, and rotator cuff
Tuesday	Off
Wednesday	Plyometrics, core
Thursday	Off
Friday	Lower body, upper body, shoulder and elbow maintenance, core, scapula, and rotator cuff
Saturday	Off
Sunday	Speed drills

Three-day split (one or two times per week for each muscle group): A three-day split trains the entire body but spreads it out over a three-day period. To train each muscle group one time per week, schedule three workout sessions per week. To hit each muscle group twice per week, double the total workouts to six for the week. One common way to break down the three-day split is to divide the upper body into two workouts and leave the lower body for its own day. One way to divide the upper body into two sessions is by training the pushing muscles (chest, shoulders, triceps) on one day and the pulling muscles (back and biceps) on another. The push/pull routine allows the muscles not being used that day to recover even when the upper body is still being trained. Table 13.2 shows an example of a push-pull-legs three-day split.

Table 13.2   Push-Pull-Legs Three-Day Training Split

Day	Area trained
Monday	Speed drills, chest, shoulders, triceps, core
Tuesday	Back, biceps, core
Wednesday	Legs, core, scapula and rotator cuff
Thursday	Off
Friday	Repeat Monday if goal is two times per week
Saturday	Repeat Tuesday if goal is two times per week
Sunday	Repeat Wednesday if goal is two times per week

PAIRING MUSCLE GROUPS

When designing a program it is important to follow a couple of guidelines. First, always perform larger–muscle group exercises before smaller–muscle group exercises. For instance, do not work the calves prior to squatting since more strength is needed for the squat. Fatiguing a smaller muscle group such as the calves before working a larger muscle group such as the quads or glutes not only inhibits the strength gains desired from the squat but also can be dangerous. Having tired legs while performing a squat is unsafe.

Second, identify weaknesses in muscle groups and try to make them a priority. Do the lifts that involve these weaker areas first. This keeps weaker areas fresh and able to work harder, which allows the weaker areas to catch up. Also, consider adding volume to the muscle groups that need improvement. Devote one entire session per week to very weak muscle groups. This allows more attention on the weak area with fresh, fully rested muscles.

Baseball players are notorious for imbalances in muscle strength due to repetitive movements in one direction (e.g., throwing and hitting). Muscle groups are balanced right to left and front to back in a healthy baseball player.

TYPES OF EXERCISES

Three to five sets of three to five different exercises are usually devoted to one muscle group. Different modes (e.g., body weight, free weights, machines) of exercise allow muscles to be worked in a variety of motions, angles, and intensities to maximize the stress placed on the muscle.

Free-weight exercises: Free-weight exercises should be used by anyone looking to gain strength. There are two basic types of free weights: barbells and dumbbells. Barbells are typically 5- to 7-foot-long bars loaded with weight on each end, whereas dumbbells are individual hand-held weights. Exercises performed with barbells and dumbbells allow for greater recruitment of stabilizing muscles (secondary muscles that assist the primary muscle) and increased range of motion, both of which afford greater strength gains and assist with injury prevention. Using free weights provides a more accurate measure of strength; a 20-pound weight is a 20-pound weight. Many machines have cables, pulleys, weight stacks, cams, and rods that often affect the true amount of weight lifted. Dumbbells are a great way to balance out the body's weaknesses. Because the dumbbell is used with a single limb, it allows an athlete to focus on any undertrained muscles, creating greater overall muscle balance.

Machine-based exercises: Machine-based weight-training exercises are a great supplement to free weights. In general, machines are very safe and can usually be used without a spotter. While machines limit the number of stabilizing muscles recruited, they also allow an athlete to push or pull harder without worrying about having to balance the weight. This in turn helps to overload the target area with ease. The Smith press machine, for example, allows an athlete to squat heavier loads without requiring the balance needed with a barbell on the back. Cable machines are another effective means of overloading muscles throughout a full range of motion, which is particularly important for baseball players.

Machine-based exercises are a safe alternative to free weights and also add variety to a program. In fact, some muscle groups are harder to train if using only free weights. Take the hamstring group for instance, one of the most often injured areas for baseball players. The number of movements possible to target this muscle group with free weights is limited. Leg curl machines and cables provide more exercises to address potential hamstring weakness.

Unilateral and bilateral exercises: Lower-body exercises can be performed using a single leg (unilaterally) or both legs (bilaterally). Unilateral lower-body exercises use body weight, dumbbells, weighted vests, or machines. Less weight is used with a unilateral leg press than when the exercise is performed bilaterally. A single-leg squat can be done with body weight alone or with an added weight vest to make it more challenging. Unilateral training challenges weaker limbs and adds variety too. Lower-body training is a great way for baseball players to correct muscle imbalances and increase overall stability and balance.

Compound and isolation exercises: A compound exercise involves multiple joints and muscles throughout the movement. The squat, lunge, step-up, and deadlift are examples of compound exercises in that they all involve flexion and extension at the ankles, knees, and hips. Isolation exercises involve movement at only one joint. An example of an isolation exercise is the leg curl (movement at the knee joint only). Because of the movement required in baseball, compound exercises are probably better suited for players who want to build size and get stronger. Isolation exercises are best for supplementing compound exercises and may be more appropriate for working around an injury or reconditioning an area after an injury.

EXERCISE ORDER

When designing a program and deciding which exercises to pair in a split, keep in mind that order is very important. Always try to do compound exercises before isolation exercises, especially if the exercises involve the same muscle group. Compound exercises use multiple muscles or muscle groups and are very taxing because of this. Plus, they are often performed with much heavier loads than isolation exercises. Take care not to fatigue muscles using isolation exercises before taking on the more difficult compound lifts. For example, avoid single-leg extensions before lunging or squatting.

Another general rule is to perform free-weight exercises before machine-based movements. It takes more balance and control to lift free weights, so coming at them fresh is the best approach. There are some exceptions to this rule, however; for example, an athlete doing heavier machine-based compound exercises, such as the leg press, and following that with free-weight seated calf raises. The isolated seated calf raise, while it is a free-weight exercise, involves only one joint (the ankle) and is not affected much by the leg press.

Along the same lines, try to place barbell exercises before dumbbell exercises. Generally barbell exercises require more weight, and extra strength is needed to move the heavier loads.

Finally, identify areas of weakness and place them earlier in the workout. This allows an athlete to work these areas when they are most rested and get the best strength gains out of the movements.

About the Authors

Mike Roberts is the business development manager at Athletes' Performance, where he directs baseball athlete relations and the sales of major league and minor league training programs. He is also the director of education for SmartKage Sports, a technology system that quantitatively measures athletic performance. A lifelong baseball coach, he is currently the head coach of the Cotuit Kettleers in the Cape Cod Collegiate Summer Baseball League. Roberts played professional baseball in the Kansas City Royals minor league system.

Roberts spent 23 seasons as head baseball coach at the University of North Carolina. Under his guidance, the team played in two College World Series championship series in Omaha and won five Atlantic Coast Conference Championships. Of his athletes, 14 have gone on to play in the major leagues, including two all-stars, B.J. Surhoff and Brian Roberts, one of the most successful base stealers in the majors. Additionally, five of his former players serve as head baseball coaches of Division I schools.

Tim Bishop owns and operates PerformFit Sports Experience, a sport performance and fitness facility, in Cockeysville, Maryland. He also creates strength and conditioning programs for Ripken Baseball's summer camps and clinics. Bishop served as the strength and conditioning coach for the Baltimore Orioles for 14 years. He also played professional baseball for the New York Yankees and, as a two-sport star, took part in the NFL training camp in St. Louis.

Bishop has appeared on numerous television and radio stations to promote health, fitness, and sport performance training. He is a frequent contributor to *Men's Health, Maximum Fitness,* and *Men's Fitness* magazines. His training advice has appeared in *New York Times, USA Today,* and *NSCA Journal.* He has lectured on a variety of topics for the Professional Baseball Athletic Trainers Society, National Strength and Conditioning Association, M-F Athletics, and various colleges and universities. In addition, he is author of *Stronger Legs and Lower Body* (Human Kinetics, 2012) and coauthor of the *Power for Sports DVD* (Human Kinetics, 2006).

Bishop has a bachelor's degree in human movement and sport studies and a master's degree in exercise science. He is a certified strength and conditioning specialist and a registered strength and conditioning coach through the National Strength and Conditioning Association.

You'll find other outstanding baseball resources at

www.HumanKinetics.com/baseball

In the U.S. call 1-800-747-4457

Australia 08 8372 0999 • Canada 1-800-465-7301
Europe +44 (0) 113 255 5665 • New Zealand 0800 222 062

 HUMAN KINETICS
The Premier Publisher for Sports & Fitness
P.O. Box 5076 • Champaign, IL 61825-5076 USA